THEOLOGY

Religion
Without Wrappings

Religion Without Wrappings

by

DAVID H. C. READ

Minister of the Madison Avenue Presbyterian Church

WILLIAM B. EERDMANS PUBLISHING COMPANY
Grand Rapids, Michigan

Printed in the United States of America

To Rory on his first birthday

Preface

Karl Barth used to say that a Christian preacher is the man with the Bible in one hand and the daily newspaper in the other.

These sermons were written with that ideal in view and are printed here as preached recently in New York City. Their content is, I hope, Biblically contemporary and their style reasonably nonprofessional. I owe a debt, not only to the theologians who have nourished me, but to my congregation who is a constant stimulus, and especially to those who have "talked back" both in public discussion and private conversation.

This book contains about a year's diet of weekly preaching and is not a selection of those "most likely to succeed." If the word must be used, let me say that the only *relevance* I have sought is that of the Gospel.

For skillful preparation of the manuscript I would thank my secretary, Carolyn Mathis.

DAVID H. C. READ

Madison Avenue Presbyterian Church
New York City

7

Contents

I

Who Plays God?

*Look unto me, and be ye saved, all the ends of
the earth: for I am God, and there is none else.*

ISAIAH 45:22

"I am God, and there is none else." We are living
in a day when there is so much "else" that it is hard
for many to hear the Voice from the depths that says:
"I am God." It was all very well, we think, for the
man of the Bible to make his splendid assertion of
God's total control over all that is, his absolute claim
on the loyalty and devotion of mankind, but he knew
nothing of the powers that have passed into human
hands in the last few hundred years. He stood in awe
before the heavens that declared the glory of God:
we penetrate them with our telescopes and plan round
trips to the moon. (The psalmist who wrote: "The
moon by night thee shall not smite" could not have
dreamed that the time would come when he might
have written: "The moon by night *thou* shalt not

11

smite.") He thought of plagues and disease as visitations from which he asked God to deliver him: we think of them as germs and bacilli to be sought out and destroyed. He thought of man's anxieties and guilt feelings as a conflict between man and his God: we think of them as a conflict between the patient and his psychiatrist. He thought that God alone could make the desert blossom as the rose: we think it can be done by fertilizers and irrigation. Above all he felt that birth and death were in the hands of God and "none else:" we are familiar with birth control and are moving into the area of death control through organ transplant and other methods of prolonging life.

Whether or not this radical change in the human situation really affects the validity of the words: "I am God, and there is none else," there is no doubt that in the popular mind the thought of God is more remote. It is as if over the last hundred years or so he had been gradually edged out of one area after another until there is left only what Julian Huxley called "the faint trace of God, half metaphysical, half magical, brooding over our world like the smile of a cosmic Cheshire cat." (Sometimes it seems as though the only prerogative left to God by modern man is the weather. And even that now seems doubtful — for every night I hear on the television that "the weather is brought to you by the Blankety-Blank Trust Company.")

Now I want you to notice that the words of our

12

text say nothing about specific areas of God's control, and I don't believe the prophet would have modified in the slightest degree the proclamation of his total sovereignty if he were living today. All—galaxies, atoms, microbes, the human brain, the enquiring spirit — are subject to the God who made them, and when it comes to our ultimate allegiance "there is none else." It's not this God who has been gradually edged out of our universe, but some idol of our creation. And I have no doubt that the prophet, looking at our world today, would have recorded with even more emphasis the words: "Look unto me, and be ye saved, all the ends of the earth."

The fact is that when belief in this God is weakened or extinguished men seek salvation in some other power. We do it today as conspicuously as any Israelite whoring after the idols of Canaan. We don't call it idolatry. We call it playing God. The dream of the old rationalists has never come true: there is no sign of a religionless society, swept clean of all belief in unseen powers, and offering no savior. On the contrary the instinct to worship is transferred elsewhere, and salvation is sought in those who assume the role of God. This is what you might call the basic temptation of mankind — to worship that which is not God and to look for deliverance from false Messiahs. This seems to me the inner meaning of the temptations of Christ as recorded in the Gospels.

It is important to note that there is nothing fundamentally evil, or necessarily corrupting, about the "something else" we are going to consider, just as there was nothing intrinsically wrong with the suggestions of the Devil in the recorded temptations. What's wrong with stones being made bread, or jumping from the pinnacle of the Temple and floating down unharmed, or with "all the kingdoms of the world, and the glory of them"? The evil appears only when what they represent is substituted for our loyalty to God. Jesus did indeed feed the multitudes; he did indeed reveal mystical powers; he did indeed make his claim upon the kingdoms of the world. But he perceived the temptation and gave his answer on our behalf: "It is written, Thou shalt worship the Lord thy God, and him only shalt thou serve."

And there is nothing fundamentally wrong, or necessarily corrupting, about the three figures that I am bringing before you from our life today. They are dangerous and corrupting only in so far as they tend to play God for modern man. They are deceiving only when they broadcast the message: "Look unto me, and be ye saved, all the ends of the earth."

(1) First, let me speak of the technocrat. By the technocrat I mean the man who controls and exploits the discoveries of modern science, the expert who applies the skills of technology to the problems of the day. More and more vital decisions are passing into

14

his hands, as the boundaries of knowledge are expanded, and the hitherto impossible comes on to the agenda. The believer should thank God for the immense gifts bestowed on us by scientific discovery and its exploitation. This is our way of turning stones into bread. Food production across the world can be immensely increased; diseases can be conquered; population can be controlled; life can be prolonged; education and the standard of living can be raised to higher levels; and the entire human race lifted nearer to that City of God of which the generations have dreamed. The trouble comes at one point only: and that is when the technocrat plays God.

Let me give you an example of what I mean. Probably the most important popular lecture series in Great Britain is that broadcast each year by the B.B.C. under the title: The Reith Lectures. The latest of these has just concluded, and I quote from the opening words of the Provost of King's College, Cambridge. "Men have become like gods. Isn't it about time we understood our divinity? Science offers us total mastery over our environment and over our destiny, yet instead of rejoicing we are deeply afraid. Why should this be?" Here is another quotation: "All of us need to understand that God, or nature, or chance, or evolution, or the course of history, or whatever you like to call it, can't be trusted any more. We simply *must* take charge of our own fate."

On this I must make two comments. First, to say that "science offers us *total* mastery over our environment and over our destiny" is nonsense, and I have never met a scientist who would make such a claim. But more important is the question as to who this "we" may be who must take charge of our fate. It cannot be the whole human race; it cannot be people like you and me who have little access to these new sources of power and control. It can only be the technocrat. Enormous powers will most surely be in his hands. Vast questions concerning the welfare and destiny of the human race will call for decision. The lecturer asked why we should be deeply afraid. What sensible person is not alarmed at the thought of decisions being taken in matters of literal life and death, decisions concerning what kind of beings are going to be bred in the future, or what span of life should be granted them, by a group of technocrats who truly believe that they must take charge of our fate? It is not the technocrat or the scientist as such of whom we are afraid. It is this breed of men who believe quite literally that their role is to exercise the powers of a God they are persuaded is defunct.

It is at this point that the Christian calls a halt. We do not plead for a restraint upon scientific experiment, but for a rejection of the claim to play God. Stones into bread? Yes, let man exploit the universe for the good of his fellows, but as man and not as God. "Thou

16

shalt worship the Lord thy God, and him only shalt thou serve." Is there any ultimate safeguard against the potential tyranny of the technocrat than this: "Look unto me, and be ye saved, all the ends of the earth: for I am God, and there is none else"?

(2) I believe it is because many are now in revolt against the thought of a technical civilization developing more and more goods and gadgets, and extending control right into the mind and soul of man, that we are now seeing a revival of the mystical, and inward search for a spirituality that knows that "man does not live by bread alone." It is this cult of the soul, this deeply personal religious experience, that I intend by the word "Yogi." I use the eastern word because the spiritual search, particularly among the young, today seems to be much more in the direction of the wisdom and the practices of revived Buddhism and Hinduism than of the mystic strain in Christianity. It is as if the Christian Church was too much identified in their minds with this technological society that is being rejected. The religious impulse drives the disillusioned technocrat and his victims into the arms of the Yogi.

And what is wrong with that? Nothing — if it is a re-awakening to the deeper dimensions of our human life. Nothing — if it brings a new awareness of the inner light that a sophisticated, materialist society had nearly extinguished. Nothing — if it means the injection into our western way of life of that spirituality,

17

that sense of the holy, that tends to evaporate here in that all-pervading secularism of our institutions — including the churches. It has, of course, at times the aspect of an escape. A purely meditative, soul-expanding, cult can be a means of avoiding our responsibilities in the social and political arena, and there are indications in, for instance, the Hippie mentality of the use of a cult as a vehicle for this kind of dropping out.

But the real temptation of the Yogi is far more subtle. In all mysticism there is a lurking tendency to deify one's own soul. The experience is sought for its own sake, for the sense of spiritual power, for the exuberance of a very private revelation. This dropout from the pinnacle of the Temple, this demonstration of spiritual power, what was it but the temptation to celebrate the self? The temptation to worship one's own soul is much more subtle than that of worshipping one's body by turning stones into bread. It is sometimes the Yogi in us, rather than the secularist, who is tempted to play God. "Look unto me, and be ye saved," cries the mystic who has lost the sense of the presence of One who says: "I am God, and there is none else." When the Yogi within us stirs to a new vision of the God of all the ends of the earth, all is well. When he concentrates entirely on the development of a private spirituality and mystic power, then he has begun to play God, and the truth is not in us.

(3) Now, what about the Church? Ideally the Church

of Jesus Christ is set in every land to proclaim this Word of the living God, to remind us of his sovereignty over every aspect of existence from our daily bread to our mystic vision, from our family plans to our flights to the moon; and to demonstrate the salvation that is found in him. Those who have responded to the grace of our Lord Jesus Christ, and the love of God, and the communion of the Holy Spirit, should be armed against any temptation to play God, and should be quick to perceive the dangers when any group, at home or abroad, assumes the mantle of divinity.

Yet we have to confess that the Church has not always resisted the temptation to identify her institutions with God himself, to act as Lord and not as Servant, and to seek for herself a dominion over "the kingdoms of the world and the glory of them". At the Vatican Council the word "triumphalism" was used to designate this tendency of the Church across the years to seek power and control, to dominate the councils of men, to win a position of prestige and glory for herself alone. And it is not the Roman Church alone that has yielded to this temptation.

Today there are few places where the Church can play God with outward pomp and privilege. But there are other ways in which we can forget that the Church is merely the servant of the Savior-God. In one direction the Church plays God today when she is too arrogant in her spiritual claims, claiming to know too much about the plans of the Almighty, drawing lines to exclude from the family of God those who do not conform exactly to her rules. A very orthodox church may be damnably unorthodox in this, usurping the prerogative of God and declaring who is, and who is not saved. In another direction, the Church plays God by seeking to intervene with directions and advice in every area of society, multiplying its pronouncements on every possible topic, and playing for power among the kingdoms of the world. A very liberal church can be quite illiberal in its treatment of dissenters from the party line. It is not accidental that this kind of playing God becomes more apparent whenever the reality of God himself is called in question.

"Get thee hence, Satan." The Lord we worship knows how powerful is the temptation we have been considering. But we remember that, as in his Cross and Resurrection, he wins this victory for us. He comes before us as the Servant-Lord who works among men in sheer dependence on his Father in heaven. And he left a Servant-Church that must always point away from herself to the same eternal God. And in it he sets men and women with various kinds of authority, but always to serve, never to play God.

Across the land today, amid the symbols of our modern might and potential, the towers and spires still point upwards to remind us of the God who is sovereign, above all human pretensions to control the future and decide our fate, beneath all depths of spirituality in which we may pride ourselves. With humble confidence the Church is here to say: "There is no substitute for the living God. There is no salvation within man himself. So will you listen through the clatter of our machines, through the silence of the soul, to the Voice that says as clearly today as in the past: 'Look unto me, and be ye saved, all the ends of the earth: for I am God, and there is none else' "?

2

Who Needs Horoscopes?

How little faith you have! And so you are not to set your mind on food and drink; you are not to worry. For all these are things for the heathen to run after; but you have a Father who knows that you need them. No, set your mind upon his kingdom, and all the rest will come to you as well.

ST. LUKE 12:29-31 (NEB)

"You have a Father." That's the core of the teaching of Jesus Christ. That's what he believed — that our human lives and destinies are in the hands of a living God who wants the best for us, as a good human father wants the best for his children. In that faith he lived day by day; and in that faith he died. For centuries men and women have found in Christ the way to this Father, and — in spite of all doubts and discouragements — have entrusted their lives to him. As the Heidelberg Confession puts it: "I trust in him so completely that I have no doubt that he will provide me with all things necessary for body and soul." Such faith has never been easy in any generation, but it has lit the way for millions, including most of the great spirits who influenced this world for good. We are surrounded by the cloud of witnesses, those who lived by faith; and they join with us every time we sing: "A mighty fortress is our God." They too tell us: "You have a Father."

And now I listen to the voice of shrewd modern observers — philosophers, dramatists, novelists, theologians — and they tell me it is all over. This is the age of science and there isn't room in it any more for this heavenly Father. No one can believe in any invisible deity presiding over the affairs of men, and in fact we have reached the point where we don't need him any more. The whole territory of the supernatural has been evacuated, and now we can get on with the business of tidying up the world without relying on any religious gimmicks. Modern man knows how things work. He has the instruments to do whatever his reason dictates. It's a rational world he lives in, and you can't fool him any longer with tales of mystery and miracle.

Strangely enough, it is some theologians who are most vociferous about the disappearance of the heavenly Father. They are absolutely certain that this is a new age where the Church cannot expect anybody to accept any belief that is not scientifically grounded, or to profess any religion except one that can be expressed in purely secular terms. They are obsessed by the notion that the average man is a rationalist who believes only what he thinks he can prove, a secularist whose vision is set on the things of this world only, and a pragmatist who judges all things by their results.

I wonder where they have been living, and what magazines they read. From what I hear and see the conviction grows that a great segment of the modern world is in full flight from the era of rationalism, secularism, and pragmatism. Never for years has there been so much discussion of the spiritual factors of life from the highest levels to the lowest. Students are flocking to courses in religion even in secular universities. Hippies are irrational, non-secular, and non-pragmatist enough to drive their elders mad. These same elders are themselves a little tired of the conventions of materialism and are turning to the writers who open the way to another dimension, or to discussions on spiritism and extra-sensory perception. The appealing figure of the age is not any more the technologist but the guru. It might even be said that there is more interest now in the journey inwards to the mystical than outwards to the moon.

On an even more popular level the swing can be detected in the fantastic proliferation of the literature of the occult. Astrology, divination, crystal-gazing, fortune-telling, palmistry, phrenology are reaching epidemic proportions. Popular magazines abound in advertisements for amulets, talismans, ouija boards, and crystal balls. Horoscopes are published by an astonishing

24

number of newspapers and periodicals. All kinds of unexpected people will talk seriously about their sign in the Zodiac, and probably far more than would admit it to their friends are influenced in their decisions by the message of the stars. And what are you to make of an "Age of Science" that constructs skyscraper hotels and hospitals which curiously have no thirteenth floor? As compared with a hundred years ago a good case could be made for calling this instead the "Age of Superstition."

Yet the word "superstition" begs too many questions. Its literal meaning is "unnecessary belief," and who is to judge another man's belief unnecessary? For quite a number of my friends my own Christian faith is a superstition, although they may be too polite to say so. There is, however, a line to be drawn between the belief that there is a God of goodness and justice whose will may be disclosed to us, and the belief that our lives are subject to the influence of the planets, or the caprice of spirits who may be placated by spells and charms. We may believe in the reality of the realm of spirit without abandoning ourselves to all kinds of fatalism, spookiness, or wizardry. I would go farther and say that *only* a strong faith in the God revealed in the Bible can preserve us from the dominion of sheer superstition — the irrational, the arbitrary, and the occult.

Let me focus on one immensely popular cult. When

25

I raise the question: "Who needs horoscopes?" I am not being haughty or sarcastic. Nor am I about to launch a diatribe against the current interest in astrology. I mean the question quite literally. Who *needs* horoscopes? Who are the people for whom this kind of belief is an absolute necessity — and why?

I can well understand how astrology can be a fascinating study. It is immensely old. It has attracted the interest of some remarkable people from the ancient Babylonians and Egyptians through Jewish and Christian Kabbalists to the semi-skeptical Chaucer, Shakespeare, and Milton. But in recent years it has been studied not only academically: Hitler and the Nazi leaders consulted astrologers and we should probably be surprised to learn who else. When you raise the inevitable question: "Is there anything in it?" I have to know what you mean. If you mean: "Is it possible that the character of men and nations is determined by the movement across the sky of lifeless lumps of volcanic matter known as planets, and that our future can be predicted by their study?" I can only answer No. For such a belief runs counter to both my reason and my religion. But if you mean: "Is there an area of human experience that may be penetrated by something other than our five senses, and are there people of psychic sensitivity who have strange adventures in space-time?" I can only answer Why not? When we descend from our ivory towers of the mind and listen to life we begin to learn that "there are more things in heaven and earth... than are dreamt of in our philosophy."

I imagine, however, that the person who regularly reads the horoscopes provided for us today has neither an academic interest in astrology, nor a passion for the psychic. The motive is probably what you might call amusement tempered with a little secret superstition — like that of the man who, when touching wood, explains that he is not superstitious but doesn't believe in taking any chances. (Incidentally I had the curiosity to look up Sunday the eleventh of February in a horoscope book under my sign of Capricorn, and read the following words: "Enjoy a good inspirational sermon." I hope all you Capricorns are enjoying yourselves!)

What does the Bible have to say about astrology and the realm of the occult? From references in both Old and New Testaments it is clear that the answer is contained in my title: Who needs horoscopes? The Bible does not give the rationalist answer which would be to deny completely the possibility of such unseen influences and psychic experiences. It recognizes the existence of those we call "mediums," and we should remember that the Wise Men in St. Matthew's story were probably Babylonian astrologers. But from beginning to end the Bible proclaims a living God who is the sole and sufficient object of our trust, the one supreme Lord over past, present, and future, and the

27

only power who can truly lead us through temptation and deliver us from evil. To put it crudely the Bible message is: "Why mess around in the dim and dangerous forecourts of the unseen world when the light is shining from the Throne itself?"

We find that Christ himself spoke passionately about the need for such a central trust in God, often using the most startling images and parables, and describing an almost unbelievable life of total reliance on the provisions of the heavenly Father. He meant to shock us by words that at times almost convey the impression that we shouldn't take any of the normal steps towards material security. But he wasn't a legislator ruling on such matters as savings and insurance; he was a poet stinging us awake to the glory of a life that ultimately rests in God like a child in the arms of his mother. He was not interested in a man's claim to believe in the existence of God. He wanted to know if he *trusted* him, had really committed his life to him for this world and the next. And he moved through his world fully conscious of the enormous pull of materialism as a practical philosophy, and equally aware of the temptation for frightened men and women to seek help and security in the twilight world of spirits. "How little faith you have! And so you are not to set your mind on food and drink; you are not to worry. For all these are things for the heathen to run after; but you have a Father who knows that you need them.

No, set your mind upon his kingdom, and all the rest will come to you as well."

"You have a Father." The inference is clear. If you trust the Father the insufferable burden of worry about your material needs will be lifted from you. And if you trust the Father you will have no need to go for guidance or assurance to the traffickers in the occult. As Isaiah put it in his day: "When they shall say unto me, Seek unto them that have familiar spirits, and unto wizards that peep, and that mutter: should not a people seek unto their God?"

So the plain answer to the question: Who needs horoscopes? is "Those who have lost their faith in the living God." Only those who have no real trust in the Father Almighty *need* such crutches to help them make their way through the perplexities and anxieties that beset us all. A Christian may study astrology, experiment with extra-sensory perception, have fun with horoscopes—but he doesn't *need* any of them. His only need is the love of God, the grace of the Lord Jesus Christ, and the fellowship of the Holy Spirit. And they are utterly sufficient in life and death. It is remarkable how, in our own day as in the past, wherever there is a decline in living religion the period of skepticism is followed by an upsurge of soothsaying and wizardry, and an epidemic of crystal balls. How right was St. Augustine when he said: "Thou hast made us for thyself, and our hearts are restless till they find their rest in thee."

29

I would say then that horoscopes are harmless — unless you need them. If you need them then you have forgotten, or never really heard, that "you have a Father." Let me make two concluding points.

(1) It is the Father of Jesus Christ who rules the future, and who offers us the grace to grow into his image. If we believe this we cannot also believe that the future is already written in the stars, and our character decided by the conjunction of planets at our birth. And this is not merely a matter of theoretical debate. What you believe about this will affect the way you live. If the world's history is already written in the stars why should I be active in the cause of justice and of peace? Why not wait for the inevitable? And if my character has been frozen in a horoscope should I not just accept my failures and my sins? But the Gospel speaks of forgiveness, of re-creation, and of new life in Christ. And it squarely puts the responsibility where it belongs. As Cassius told his friend:

"The fault, dear Brutus, is not in our stars,
But in ourselves, that we are underlings."

"Set your mind upon his kingdom, his rule," said Jesus. The rule of the Father extends into the dark recesses of the future, and the rule of the Father can be a mighty transforming power in your life and mine right now. To begin and end each day setting our mind on him is the most healthful exercise any of us can take.

30

(2) Then it is the Father of Jesus Christ who alone can deliver us from evil. When the real storms come upon a man or a nation we learn who is "our refuge and our strength, a very present help in trouble." There is no other Savior. This is what the prophet meant by his biting words to the Babylonians: "Let now the astrologers, the stargazers, the monthly prognosticators, stand up, and save thee from these things that shall come upon thee." When the chips are down, that is, we know that there is only one God to deliver us.

Frankly I wish there were a little more compassion in the words of the prophet, something of the spirit in which Christ wept over the city of Jerusalem. The Church is not here to denounce all other cults. The preacher is not here to condemn his fellow men who are groping for light, and hungry for hope. We are here, in response to Christ's command, to celebrate and to offer his Gospel. And at the heart of the Gospel is a simple message that can turn night into day, and carry us through whatever lies ahead: "You have a Father."

3

Too Much Talk?

...Concerning Jesus of Nazareth, which was a prophet mighty in deed and word before God and all the people.

ST. LUKE 24:19

Do you ever get the impression that we are drowning in a sea of words? Newspapers, magazines, reports, reviews, radio, television, dialogues, discussions pour in on us in a verbal torrent no other generation has ever known. At the mere flick of a switch transistorized words are available any moment of the day or night. When a crisis threatens diplomats appear on our living room screens talking by the hour, and industrial disputes are settled — or not settled — by talk marathons that run through days and nights. Cascades of words reach us from every side of social and political disputes until we hardly know what we are hearing. Then along comes Marshall McLuhan to tell us — in a hundred thousand words — that it doesn't really matter, for "the medium is the message."

Yet the effects of this verbal inflation are with us. Words are devalued. They are losing power. If I were to say to you: "Here is an important message," I have to remember that you are conditioned to expect that what follows will be a completely trivial recommendation of some cigarette or detergent. We have learned to discount "epoch-making," "sensational," and "unforgettable," as applied to books and movies, and have learned to interpret "sizzling," and "scorching." More serious is the way in which serious debate is muffled by the verbal symbols that are used. Those of us who are agonizing about the Vietnam war are not helped by the fluffy words and phrases employed by both the Administration and its harshest critics. On the one hand we hear of "containment," "pacification," "resisting aggression," "defending our liberties"; on the other about "escalation," "power structures," "genocide," "arrogance of power"; and with neither is it easy to penetrate through the words to the meaning. Our hearts sink when we contemplate more months of intensified bombardment by the cliches of this debate, and we long for a truce in the mutual reviling so that men of skill and integrity could get together to find the sanest answer, the word of power that cuts through to the truth and leads to action. Those of us who make no claim to have such an answer can at least make our plea for a slogan-pause, and epithet-armistice, and a common search for truth.

Do we talk too much? One of my first impressions when returning home after five years in a prison camp was that everyone was talking, talking, talking, about nothing in particular. We had, without realizing it, gradually eliminated all unnecessary chatter. We spoke only to communicate information, or when we deliberately wanted a discussion to pass the time. I see now that talk is a lubricant in a society where we don't know each other well. Two people in love don't need to talk very much, and in heaven, according to the Book of Revelation, "there was silence for half an hour." It may be that the torrent of words in which we live is a symptom of our lack of real communication and our devalued verbal currency a screen to shield us from the truth. I would remind you that the verse in the psalm which we like to interpret with the words "Drop thy still dews of quietness," is more correctly translated: "Shut up! and know that I am God."

I do believe that the remedy for our bewilderment and cynicism, our sense of drowning in slogans and half truths, our inability to really hear one another, does lie in the recovery of God's presence, God's Kingdom in our midst. For the pause in which we become aware of him is the entrance into the realm of truth where Yea is Yea and Nay Nay and we know one another as children of the Father. The silent Word of God that meets us when we are quiet is the silencing Word that stills the clamor of our passions so that we can hear the truth. None of us has got very far into this Kingdom, but if I did not believe it is there to be found I would not be standing here. And every now and then there is the joy of knowing that yet another has found his or her way to the entrance in response to Christ's invitation: "Come unto me and I will give you rest" — which means just that, rest from the self-justifying clamor of our human words.

But how can the Church effectively declare and communicate this Good News? For it seems we are in this business of words. We've used them ever since we entered this building today in hymns and prayers and readings, and I am using them now. And I doubt if anyone dropping in to our worship from an alien world would find that we were any less victims of the devalued word, the meaningless slogan, and the tired cliche than anybody else. Aren't we Presbyterians in particular, with our emphasis on the Bible and on preaching, wordmongers to the highest degree? A Roman Catholic may look, a Quaker may sit in silence, but you have to listen. The title of my sermon was given me by a four year old, the son of a minister friend in the Church of Scotland, who was attending his first church service. His mother watched him anxiously as the service proceeded. He sat silently for about half an hour and then suddenly and audibly gave his verdict on the proceedings: "Too much talk!"

Let's admit it. We probably use too many words —

and often not the right words — in our worship. We could use more silence. We could express more in symbol, in movement, and in rhythm. Let's also admit that human words can never convey the reality of God in neat packages of logic. And let's admit that a church whose words have no resonance in the daily life and decisions of its members is a "sounding gong and a tinkling cymbal." Let's agree even with those who write long books to prove that words are useless if we're not "where the action is."

Then let us note that in every age, including this, God has used the stumbling words of men in prayer and praise and preaching to convey the silent Word of his Kingdom, and the living Word who is his Christ. The Bible which, in one sense, is a very odd collection of ancient words — arranged into stories, poems, letters, images, vision — has proved to be the Book with unique power to bring the silent Word to life in men's hearts, the Word that silences our chatter and confronts us with our God. And the sermon that derives its authority from this Bible, no matter how choked it may be with foolish words, empty words, obscure words, or just altogether too many words, can still, by the grace of God, open the door to his Kingdom for the man or woman of today.

What I mean by the silent Word is the divine presence, the divine power that reaches us through or, if you like, underneath the human words that we hear.

Too Much Talk?

I once attended a service when I was a student of
which I can remember not a word. It was not my own
church; the form of worship was not to my taste; and
the sermon in no way remarkable. Yet in that service
the silent Word so reached me that in my plans for a
career I was stopped in my tracks. Suddenly, and
completely unexpectedly, I knew that I had to become
a minister. This was no earth-shaking event, but at
least it has given me the confidence that even through
what St. Paul calls "the foolishness of preaching" still
today the silent Word can change the lives of people
like you and me.

Did you hear the description of Jesus Christ given
in that extraordinary last chapter of St. Luke's Gospel?
"A prophet mighty in deed and word." There is no
suggestion in the Gospels that the words of Jesus were
considered less important than his deeds. No one said:
"Let's have less of this God-talk and more healing of
the sick and feeding of the hungry." Instead we read
at the end of the Sermon on the Mount that "the
people were astonished at his doctrine: for he taught
them as one having authority, and not as the scribes."
The mighty word and the mighty deed were insepar-
able. When they brought a paralytic to him for cure,
and his first words were "Thy sins be forgiven thee,"
there were some who thought that this was mere talk,
just as many today blame the Church for chattering
about sin and forgiveness instead of tackling the ills of

society. His comment was: "Is it easier to say 'Thy sins be forgiven thee'; or to say, 'Arise, and take up thy bed, and walk'?" Of course it's easier to *say*: "Thy sins be forgiven thee," if this is mere talk. But suppose it isn't? Suppose the forgiveness of sins is as real a fact, and as desperate a need as the healing of the body? For Jesus it was. "That ye may know that the Son of man hath power on earth to forgive sins ... I say unto thee, Arise, and take up thy bed, and walk." And it happened. *Both* happened. The word of forgiveness was as mighty as the act of healing. Do we believe that?

The silent Word, the Word of God that speaks through such human language, is a Word of power. When we have the impression that there is too much talk in the Church today and not enough action we could be right. But the answer is not to turn away from prayer and worship and the proclamation of the Gospel in order to get busy out there where the action is. If we are not hearing and obeying the silent Word how shall we know what to do when we get there? What we need is the Word with power. For such a word is never to be separated from action. When the Word with power finds lodgment in the heart of a worshipping man or woman something happens. And that something will sooner or later pass over into action. In the language of the Old Testament, and in the language that Jesus spoke, one single sound con-

veyed both meanings: "Word" and "Deed." It may
be that St. Luke had to use two Greek words for the
one that was used by the disciple who spoke of Jesus
of Nazareth "mighty in deed and word." In Biblical
thinking the one could be as powerful as the other. A
true Word *did* something. Such a creative Word lay
behind the very emergence of the universe. "And God
said, Let there be light: and there was light." "In the
beginning was the Word."

It is this Word that we seek in worship, this Word
of power that we are listening for when the minister
says: "Hear the Word of God." It assures us that
everything is not just confusion, and that we are not
drowning in a sea of idle chatter. It can renew our
conviction that there is a truth to be sought and found
amid the chaos of conflicting opinion. It expands our
souls so that we are not hemmed in by the limits of
human language, and frees us from the isolation that
mere human chatter cannot penetrate. Here is the
Word of power that Christ still offers, as the crucified
and risen Lord, "mighty in deed and word." "Come
unto me."

It is not sheer convention that makes me speak at
this point of Christ and his cross. For the one who impressed his contemporaries as a "prophet mighty in
deed and word," has impressed the whole world by his
sacrificial love. It is in him that we discover the deepest
truth of all — that the silent Word, the Word of God,

39

is not only a Word of power. It is a Word of compassion. It brings from the unseen world not only the knowledge of God's presence, but the assurance of his love. The Word made flesh in Jesus Christ speaks of an infinite care and compassion for every human life ever born into this world. "God so loved the world that he gave his Son" — but that "world" was no abstraction. It was the paralytic. It was Mary Magdalene. It was Peter. It was Zacchaeus. It was the man on the corner of Madison Avenue. It was you.

The Bible is full of names, not abstractions. The Word of God comes concretely — to people — and it comes with compassion. Two fascinating stories, one from the Old Testament and one from the New, make this gloriously clear.

Here's Elisha the prophet. A prophet is a preacher, a dealer in words. And Elisha probably suggests to you a thunderer with words. Israel's prophets were always blasting away whether they were heeded or not. And the general opinion of the average citizen about the prophets may well have been: "Too much talk." Today, if we read them, we may feel overwhelmed by their eloquence, and somewhat mystified by their drift. Then and now, however, there is no doubt that the sensitive ear can detect the Word behind their words — the silent Word of power. But is that all?

There are few more moving stories in the Bible or elsewhere than this one of the Shunammite and her little boy, the boy she had prayed for and doted on. And the whole prophetic action seems to stop while Elisha concentrates on this little boy. For he has had a heat stroke in the field and has collapsed. It is as if for Elisha now only one thing matters. The word of power that he has to declare to kings and councils becomes a word of compassion to a little boy and his sorrowing mother. The Word of God is now focussed on the lifeless body; and the prophet of God is stretched out in what we would surely call "mouth-to-mouth resuscitation." "And the flesh of the child waxed warm." How intensely vivid and human it is. "And the child sneezed seven times, and the child opened his eyes." That's how the Bible speaks. And that's how the Word we hear today must be interpreted. When Elisha preached men heard the voice of God, but the Word had never greater power than when it was the Word of compassion, and he turned to this mother and said: "Take up thy son."

And here is St. Paul, the apostle. Surely an apostle is a preacher, a dealer in words. His was the voice that stirred the ancient world from Damascus to Rome. His were the books that were to be read for two thousand years. Yet here again the Bible surprises us with a little story of sheer humanity and compassion.

"Too much talk" must certainly have been the verdict when St. Paul was preaching at Troas. It was an evening service, St. Luke tells us, and in a stuffy room the sermon went on till midnight. The inevitable happened. Someone fell asleep — and simultaneously fell from the top gallery of the room. Only the Bible would include a story like this in an account of a great spiritual leader. If St. Paul was possessed only by this Word of power that was in him he might just have signalled the ushers to remove the body while he continued to preach. Some of his detractors believe that this is just the kind of fanatic he was. But again the Word was compassion and focussed for the moment entirely on that one wretched youth lying prone on the ground floor. And is there any mighty thunder in the Epistles that is more the Word of God than this: "Paul went down, and fell on him, and embracing him said, Trouble not yourselves; for his life is in him."?

A church is not a talking-shop. Neither is it merely an action group. It is a community where a very varied group of people, of all ages and types, set themselves under the rule of him who was "mighty in deed and word," and seek to be conformed to his image. In a world full of bewildering talk we seek to hear the Word of power: in the "lonely crowd," we listen to the Word of compassion. That is why we are here.

4

Uneasy Sanctuaries

I know thy works: behold, I have set before thee an open door, and no man can shut it; for thou hast a little strength, and thou hast kept my word, and hast not denied my name.

REVELATION 3:8

Since we are moving into the high season of opinion polls, surveys, and statistics, let me give you a reliable, and rather surprising, estimate concerning the Church. On any Sunday morning in the U. S. A. a higher proportion of the population is to be found in the sanctuaries of religion than in any sizable nation in the modern world, and a higher proportion than was there a hundred years ago.

And the response to such a piece of information is almost unanimous: So what? The cynical observer knows exactly how to interpret these figures. It is surprising how many claim today to be able to read the minds and the motives of those who go to church. Church attendance holds up in the United States, we are told, because worried people need reassurance; because affluent people like the status quo; because confused people look for simple solutions; because mass-conditioned people like to conform; because frightened people seek a sanctuary. The last thing that occurs to the critics is that some may go to church because they believe in Jesus Christ and want to worship God. The word they pounce on is "sanctuary." The Church is the religious hideaway. Here they can find the old familiar things; here they can forget for a restful hour the clamoring problems of every day; here they can be soothed with soft music and drugged with holy words and sent away persuaded that all is well. No wonder, the critic says, the sanctuary still holds up: they need it, especially the older ones who can still remember what security felt like.

It's time this neat little theory was confronted with the facts. If there ever was a time when the churches offered this kind of sanctuary it is certainly not now. And if there is any part of the country where the Church is a stable, smug, conventional, successful purveyor of religious sedatives, it is certainly not New York. The characteristic of American churches today is restlessness and self-criticism rather than stability and assurance. The idea of the Church as a network of amiable and undisturbed sanctuaries of comfort is sheer myth. The indications are that many of those who make up this precarious high-water-mark of church

44

attendance are anything but settled and secure in their beliefs and hopes. And clear across the country there is a deep uneasiness about the message and the mission of the Christian Church.

Uneasy sanctuaries — that's what we have today. The uneasiness stems from at least two factors in the present situation.

(1) There is the turmoil in theology and worship. Just when the Church seemed to be the one place left where you could be sure of finding ancient truths and moral standards reaffirmed, suddenly everything seems to be called in question. Just when the Church seemed to be the one place left where the old rituals could still be found, suddenly everything is in the melting pot. Even the most venerable and traditionalist religious institutions are now in flux, and we watch with startled fascination the heresies of a bishop or the hemline of a nun. The uneasiness has been compounded by the emergence of the clergy as questioners and innovators. Doubts and rebelliousness were always in order for the layman, but he liked to feel that at least the fellow up there in the pulpit, or bent before the altar, knew what he believed, and would stick to the book. It is unsettling to feel that one's secret doubts may be voiced from the pulpit, and that the guardians of the liturgy may break loose in wild experiment and innovation. If you add to that the trend towards political activism and the rejection of traditional piety —

what I might call the theology of the picket line —
then no one can speak about sanctuaries today as
havens of peace in a world of tumultuous change.

(2) But there is another, still deeper, cause of uneasiness. Those who, in such considerable numbers,
remain loyal to this bewildering Church of the 1970's
are by no means the smug, self-satisfied group they
are accused of being. Anyone with a finger on the
pulse of a living congregation today knows how many
are dissatisfied with their own performance as Christians and conscious of the failures of their church. In
my experience it's often the man outside the Church
who is the Pharisee today. At least I've never heard a
church member say: "I thank God that I'm not like
my pagan neighbor," while I have often heard the
equivalent of "I reckon that I'm as good as, or better
than, old so-and-so for all his church-going." There's
a profound uneasiness among many about the quality
of their faith in practice, how much difference it
makes in the decisions of daily life. We've all been
asking ourselves, for instance, how this vast church-
going, Bible-hearing, Christ-honoring group to which
we belong could not have done more to stem the tide
of bigotry, racial prejudice, lawlessness, and violence
which has brought us to this critical hour. We've asked
ourselves why our churches have not been more effec-
tive instruments of true evangelism — really penetrat-
ing the society in which they are placed and minister-

ing to men's needs. This uneasiness comes to the surface in the questions we ask: "What can I do? What can our church do to be of real help in this time of crisis?" We come to the sanctuary and we receive the grace of God; but that does not mean that we go away with our doubts answered and our consciences drugged. Wherever there is a true meeting with the living Christ these are uneasy sanctuaries in our land today.

Now I want to ask if this is a reason for dismay and lamentation. If we take the long view I think we shall find that from the very beginning the Church has been healthiest when Christians have been most uneasy. Christ, you will remember, offered no securities for his followers except the care and concern of the heavenly Father. They were to live in a dangerous world — as sheep among wolves. They were to be the restless ones, always facing the question: "What do you *more* than these?" They were to be prepared for all kinds of divisions and controversies. They were to expect opposition and learn to live with confusion. It has been pointed out that this closing command does not read: "Go ye into all the world — and relax." Surely part of the meaning of that stern word about "taking up the Cross" and following is that we make up our minds to live with the uneasiness of being a Christian.

"Uneasy sanctuaries" spread the Gospel across the ancient world: "uneasy sanctuaries" produced a St. Francis; then a Luther; then a Wesley; then every

47

lively movement of reform to our own day. From Old
Testament times till now a secure, stable, undisturbed
and unruffled Church has meant spiritual death. That's
why the prophet Amos came thundering to the sleek
establishment of his day: "Woe to them that are at
ease in Zion!" That's why Jesus stung the consciences
of the comfortable with his demand that eyes be
opened to the misery of a neighbor, and ears sensitive
to the call for compassion. And that's why the Bible
gives us these sharp letters to the young churches of
Asia Minor that are to be found in the opening
chapters of that strange book known as the "Revelation". If you think there was no uneasiness, no cause
for alarm, no need for self-criticism in this glorious
dawn of the Christian Church, then read through these
letters. Unlike the letters of St. Paul these come to us
in the vivid and unfamiliar language of apocalyptic, but
the message is unmistakable: To each church the risen
Lord is pictured as appearing with words of reproof and
encouragement.

Here is the one that I found speaking to our uneasiness today. "And to the angel of the church in
Philadelphia write" — for Philadelphia it is not difficult to read New York! — "These things saith he that
is holy, he that is true, he that hath the key of David,
he that openeth, and no man shutteth; and shutteth,
and no man openeth; I know thy works: behold, I have
set before thee an open door, and no man can shut it;

for thou hast a little strength, and hast kept my word, and hast not denied my name."

"I know thy works." It is the presence of the risen Christ that really disturbs his Church. Whenever we settle down to a religious routine, content to be doing more or less what our forefathers did; whenever we find ourselves content with nominal commitment and statistical well-being; then Christ appears saying: "I know your works. I know just what your discipleship amounts to. I know. I don't despise what you are and what you are doing. For you have a little strength, and you have kept my word, and have not denied my name. But, behold!" — and with that word he always awakens the drowsy — "behold, I have set before you an open door, and no man can shut it."

When spiritual uneasiness comes to an individual or a church two things can happen. Either we seek to get rid of it by withdrawing from the struggle and finding some physical or mental drug to relieve our awakened conscience; or else we accept it as a challenge to new life and hope. I believe that the present uneasiness in our sanctuaries, and in our own souls, is driving some to the sedatives of cynical detachment or the defeatism that sees no future for living religion in the nation, the world, or in themselves. But it is impelling others to rise up and pass through that open door. For the great Christian discovery is that it is through doubts and confusions that we reach a stronger faith; through an awakened conscience we find forgiveness; and through uneasiness we reach the one true peace.

George Herbert has a poem in which he describes the Creator pouring out a glass of blessings on man — strength, beauty, wisdom, honor, pleasure. But he keeps back rest and peace. Let him keep all the others, he says:

> "But keep them with repining restlessness:
> Let him be rich and weary, that at least,
> If goodness lead him not, yet weariness
> May toss him to my breast."

At the heart of Christianity lies the supreme uneasiness of the Cross. Yet from that fearful dislocation comes the ultimate faith in the goodness and loving purpose of God. So it is that in our uneasiness, and in the uneasiness of the churches today, there can be light of faith and hope that points us through that open door to new avenues of service to God and man. What I am saying is that our uneasy sanctuaries today can be the springboards for a revival of faith and renewal of the Church. It is no disaster that fundamental matters of belief are being openly debated and accepted doctrines questioned. It may be that many of us have to pass through the uneasiness, even the agony, of questioning our faith before we can really learn what it means to trust in the Christ by whose name we are called. It is no disaster that there is an upheaval in forms of worship, and conflicting opinions about social action in the churches at this time. For from such controversy, if held in love, can come creative movements with stronger impact on the basic problems of society. Christ looks at us, his family here in this city, and says: "I know your works ... you have a little strength, and have kept my word, and have not denied my name. Behold, I have set before you an open door." Thank God if you are uneasy; for from that uneasiness I believe we shall find together not only a stronger faith, but new ways of serving the needs of this city in its hour of need.

Now let me return to the word with which we began. Sanctuary. There are some who are so enamored of the restless Church, so eager to translate the faith entirely in terms of social action, so contemptuous of anything called piety or devotion, that they would reject the notion of "sanctuary" altogether. They would like to abolish this gathering in sanctuaries for worship and have the Church dispersed in the secular world to work for radical changes in our society. I can well see how the urgent needs of our day make many impatient with the sanctuaries where we gather to pray and sing and listen to the words of the Bible. I can well see how tempting it is to hurl the charge of irrelevance at our worship here when war and slums, riots and oppression, dishonesty, bigotry, and hate demand the response of every man or woman of goodwill.

But I would ask this question. Is there anything more relevant for the Body of Christ on earth than to worship the God whom he reveals and to seek the grace by which alone both individuals and society can truly be redeemed? Is there anything more relevant for a divided and despairing world than the spiritual power that flows from the reconciling love of God? I know that such words can be used to justify a false piety that refuses action in the secular world. But is there not right now a crying need for the true piety that finds in the Gospel, of the crucified and risen Christ the real dynamic for action in the secular world? We shall undoubtedly be asked to participate as a congregation in the near future in many plans for tackling the immense problems of this city and I believe we shall respond. But the success of these very plans depends on a renewal of our faith in the living Christ, and a worship that opens us to the will of God and the reception of his grace.

The sanctuary stands with its door open. And the word inscribed on this side is "Go ye into all the world." But on the outside the word is "Come... come ye unto me." I believe the time has come when that note has to be sounded again. Has the Church in action in the world anything to offer that is not offered by other bodies similarly engaged? Surely it is the invitation to come to the Source of spiritual power and ultimate meaning. It would be tragic if, just when the signs are that this generation is again hungry for the transcendent, the expansion of consciousness, the ultimates, the churches should turn away from the sanctuary and become indistinguishable from any other movements of progress and reform. The word "sanctuary contains the word "holy", and a Church from which the holy has disappeared has betrayed her Lord.

To sum up in the language of today: Sanctuaries: Yes; Comfortable? No. It is in the uneasy sanctuaries that the Spirit of God can work.

5

Soul Transplant Next?

I am crucified with Christ: nevertheless I live; yet not I, but Christ liveth in me; and the life which I now live in the flesh I live by the faith of the Son of God, who loved me, and gave himself for me.

GALATIANS 2:20

When the news broke that a human heart had been successfully transplanted our first response was of astonishment, gratitude, and hope. This was a break-through in medical science and marked another stage in the battle against premature death. We could only marvel at the confidence and skill that made such an operation possible and pray for its success.

Then, I think, we began to realize that this is something very different from the kind of experiment or operation we are used to hearing about. These mean the tracking down of germs, or the cutting away of infected tissue, or other operations performed on a single human being. This time two human beings are involved. One gives, and another receives. Questions arise which are not simply within the province of medical science. Where do we draw the line between life and death? Who has the right to dispose of the organs of another person? At what point could the transfer of the member of one person to another conceivably lead to a switch of personality? If I were to donate my body at the point of death and almost every organ from the kidneys to the brain were transplanted into you, would you in any sense then become me?

When I saw the interview with Dr. Christiaan Barnard of Capetown it was evident that he is fully aware of the ethical and religious problems opened up by the new operation, and he spoke convincingly about its morality as well as its brilliant prospects. But the implications remain a puzzle to us all. One fringe benefit seems already secured. Now that a colored man's heart is beating away inside the skin of the white South African, we may hope to hear less of the racist nonsense that denies the fundamental kinship of the entire human family. When we have anatomical integration the arguments for social segregation become thinner than ever. Now we have a living demonstration of the solidarity of the race and the inter-dependence of all people. This man is a walking exegesis of the text: "We are members one of another."

Suppose we range to the outer extremities of the possible. I keep hearing the question: "What happens if one man's brain is transplanted into another person?" Admittedly at the moment such a question is purely hypothetical, but who today is going to be confident that the incredible may not happen? A thorough-going materialist would have to say that if you have my brain then you become me, for he believes that there is nothing to be considered but the material substance of the brain. But most of us believe that our personality, the conscious self, cannot be located exclusively in the tissues within our heads. Quite apart from any belief we have as to the survival of the person after the brain is dead we realize here and now that there is an "I" that can never be tracked down and analyzed by any instrument whatever. For whoever is observing our personality is also a person. Someone may be observing him observing me. And someone else — but I needn't go on, for this is the mystery of the self — the one part of us that can never be located and defined.

It is this "I", the center of our personality, that the Bible calls the soul. When the materialist says that no surgeon and no biologist, when examining a human body, has ever found a trace of this "soul" he is perfectly correct. For the soul is untraceable by any instrument of science. Yet, so far from being imaginary, it is the very essence of our being. When the doctor says: "I will examine your lungs," we know what lungs are, but we cannot begin to describe this "I". And yet it is the most important factor of all. The Church has often confused people by talking as if the soul were a little department tucked away somewhere inside labeled: "For religion only." There is no such department. The soul is *you;* the soul is *me.* And it is our entire being that religion is concerned with.

If this is so then even an exchange of brains, whatever it might do to the personality (and that is another matter to give us pause) could not possibly mean an exchange of self. For that would mean a transplanting of the soul, which is a meaningless phrase, since the soul, the self, is not available to the surgeon's knife. It is, of course, the province of psychology, but I doubt if any psychiatrist would claim that such a switch of personality is conceivable. For the ultimate self must always elude scientific investigation.

Let's forget any crude notion of transplanting the soul, and think now about this mysterious self and how it grows. I've not been wasting your time (I hope) with the question of organ-transplant, for it offers a kind of parable through which the Gospel may come alive for us today. Just as a man's heart can be transplanted into another, so in the invisible relationship of soul with soul, a kind of spiritual transplanting can take place. We call it influence — literally the flowing in of one self to another. It's happening all the time, whether we are aware of it or not. Sometimes the influence of one personality, especially at what we call formative

57

times, can be enormous. In a recent motion picture one can watch the influence, the flowing in, of the personality of a teacher, Miss Jean Brodie, on a group of Edinburgh schoolgirls. It is so powerful that you could almost talk about the "transplanting of the soul." From our earliest years this "self" of ours has been exposed to influence of every kind — parents, teachers, friends, the great personalities we admire, and the impact of other minds through books, music and art. And it is happening still. There is nothing static about the soul. Unless we have become spiritually dead we are constantly absorbing what others give, and we are being inwardly changed. If we are spiritually alive it is happening now.

Why are we here? The stated purpose of this church is to "bring men and women into the transforming presence of Christ, in the fellowship of the Spirit, that they may be made over in his likeness." Very simply, we are here — instead of doing something else — because we believe that the best influence of all for our lives, the flowing-in that we most desire, is that of Jesus Christ. For he brings to the very center of our being the goodness and the mercy of God, and he can work in the soul that transformation we long for — making us more like him. Every one of us here probably understands this differently. There is no one way in which the influence of Christ comes to a human life. But, as I read the New Testament, it strikes me that the deeper we penetrate into the Christian faith the stronger the language we need to describe this "influence" of Christ. What could be just a vague admiration for his person and teaching, passes into a sense of friendship and of love. And that becomes in turn what can only be described as a communion with him. And that communion is nothing less than an intimate union of soul with soul, a transplanting of his life into ours so that we realize the meaning of the words: "Abide in me, and I in you."

No one had ever a more vivid sense of this union with Christ than the apostle Paul, and no one found stronger words with which to express it. In the very depth of his being he identified himself with his Lord, believing that his old sinful self died with him on the Cross, and that his new self shared the power of his Resurrection. He had known the "transforming presence." It had turned his life upside down. And now he stated the core of his belief in these tremendous words: "I am crucified with Christ: nevertheless I live; yet not I, but Christ liveth in me; and the life which I now live in the flesh I live by the faith of the Son of God, who loved me, and gave himself for me."

Some of us may feel daunted by such words. We may say: "This intensity of faith is not for me. Mystical talk like this goes right over my head." Or we may want to ask: "What is this crucifixion of the self? Am I being asked to obliterate the very thing that makes me me, and to lose my identity in some heavenly vision? Is this what the hymn means when it says:

" 'Till in the ocean of thy love,
    We lose ourselves in heaven above'?"

Let me remind you that St. Paul was a very practical person, capable, for instance, of taking charge of a ship in a storm when sailors and soldiers were paralyzed with fear. He is simply telling us the secret of his faith — which is nothing other than the influence, the flowing in, of Christ the crucified and risen Lord. And he is by no means teaching the obliteration of the personality, the death of the self. "I am crucified with Christ: *nevertheless I live.*" We entirely misunderstand this Gospel if we think that receiving Christ makes us less individual, not unique, less a real *person* than before. The astonishing thing about the record of Christian saints from St. Paul onwards is their variety. Each one of them would have spoken of his union with Christ. Each one would have known this submission to his Lordship. Yet each one became a totally different personality — more different, more truly an individual, than if he had never known this inflowing of the Spirit and I believe this discovery of our true selves goes on beyond this life, so that it would be better to sing:

"Till in the ocean of thy love,
    We *find* ourselves in heaven above."

60

The more a man or woman is truly united with Christ the more real and strong the personality. If we ask how this can possibly be, since apparently one person is being invaded by another, the answer lies in the freedom that Christ brings to forget ourselves — and thereby find ourselves. You remember that when he issued his invitation with the words: "If any man will come after me, let him deny himself, and take up his cross daily, and follow me," he added these unforgettable words: "For whosoever will save his life shall lose it: but whosoever will lose his life, for my sake, the same will save it." The word "life" here is the word "soul." And he is plainly telling us that the way to find the soul is to forget it, and the way to develop our personality is to lose it in Christ.

Strange though it may seem this principle works in every area of life. The great ball player is not the one who is concentrating on himself and wondering all the time how he is making out, but the one who loses himself in the game. The great pianist is not the one who sits there, consciously projecting his personality across the footlights, but one who is lost in his music. And the strong personalities that we know are not the ones who send away for little booklets telling them how to win friends and influence people, but men and women who get on with the job and never give their "image" a passing thought. Those who have made their mark throughout history have been without exception the people who got lost in some cause or vision far greater than themselves — and so found themselves.

This is why we must take care that our religion doesn't bcome a constant introspection, a fussing about our souls. For Jesus obviously the soul was immensely important — "What shall a man give in exchange for his soul? — but you never find him advising people to go away and cultivate their souls. Instead he sent them off to heal the sick, to feed the hungry, to do justly, to love mercy, and to walk humbly with their God. We come to worship because we know how much our souls matter, how important it is that we should be set straight at the very center of our being. But this is no gathering of introverted soul-searchers. When worship is alert and alive we are caught up into that which is far greater than we are; we lose ourselves in the adoration of our God and the summons to love our neighbors as ourselves.

So what matters most when we come together, or when we kneel by ourselves in prayer, is that we should realize this influence, this inflowing, this indwelling of Christ. If this is what we honestly seek, if this is what we sincerely ask for in the depth of our souls, then it will happen. The spiritual transplantation will go on until, to use the apostle's words: "Christ be formed in us." It will be no more a conscious process than that of the influence of your home and friends upon you. But it will mean a sharpening of our vision for others' needs, a lessening of the grip of selfish passion, and an unselfconscious increase of faith and hope and love.

It is Christ who offers himself to us again in the simple service of the bread and wine. They speak of his crucifixion when our sins were nailed upon him, and buried with him in the tomb. They speak of his Resurrection when he came upon his disciples with the offer of new life for the world. And they speak of his Presence here and now. To receive them is to enact our deepest prayer, that our souls may be lost in him so that they be truly found, and that we be made over in his likeness. Whatever may lie ahead for you this week, at the moment of communion you will have made or renewed the strengthening and sustaining contact that enables you to say: "I am crucified with Christ: nevertheless I live; yet not I, but Christ liveth in me; and the life which I now live in the flesh I live by the faith of the Son of God, who loved me, and gave himself for me."

6

The Grip of the Familiar

*And they told what things were done in the way, and
how he was known of them in breaking of bread.*

ST. LUKE 24:35

Here is an extract from the longest, and in many
ways the most fascinating, of the few records we have of
an encounter between the Risen Christ and his disciples.
The two who walked from Jerusalem to Emmaus on
Easter afternoon are anonymous. They represent those,
like us, whose names are not inscribed in the inner
circle of the apostles. We are thus reminded that there
were many disciples, close followers of Jesus besides the
twelve familiar names. It was to the inner circle — now
twelve minus one — that these two are now reporting
back. As we read in a modern version: "Then they gave
their account of the events of their journey and told
how he had been recognized by them at the breaking
of the bread."

It was an extraordinary story. They had been joined
on their walk by a mysterious stranger. He had asked
what they were discussing and why they looked so
worried. Then they had poured out to him the story
about their friendship with Jesus of Nazareth and how

he had just been condemned to death and crucified. "We had been hoping," they said, "that he was the man to liberate Israel." Then they had told him about the rumors of a resurrection. The stranger had listened, and then he had begun to talk. As the miles went past he had expounded their scriptures — the law and the prophets — and they had begun to see how indeed this Jesus could have been the promised Liberator. Then they had stopped for a meal. "When he had sat down with them at table," we read, "he took the bread, and said the blessing; he broke the bread, and offered it to them." This had been the moment of truth. Suddenly they had realized who he was. "Their eyes were opened, and they recognized him."

That was the story they related to the apostles back in Jerusalem. It has been sealed into the memory of the Church because it conveys across the centuries with pictorial power the two ways in which the living Christ makes himself known to his anonymous disciples — in Word and in Sacrament. You cannot miss the implications of the story. He "expounded the Scriptures," and "he took bread, and blessed it, and brake, and gave to them." But today I want simply to focus on one side light in the story. Let me raise the question: How was it that, at this precise moment when they sat at the table, "their eyes were opened and they recognized him."?

Naturally, there is a mystery about this recognition — just as there is a mystery about the recognition of Christ by a man or woman today. In this and other parishes I have served when someone has come to tell me how the Christian Gospel has become real and vital, I have always been curious about how it happened. Was it the influence of a friend, an experience in prayer or worship, a word in a sermon — or what? Again and again, I am forced to realize that, whatever may spark a concern about religion, there is always an element of mystery about Christ's revelation of himself. "The wind bloweth where it listeth, and thou hearest the sound thereof, but canst not tell whence it cometh, and whither it goeth: so is every one that is born of the Spirit."

Yet here I am going to suggest that the mystery of their recognition was linked to a familiar gesture. Let's assume these were disciples who had often eaten meals with Jesus in the previous months. Everyone of us has a characteristic way of cutting a loaf (before we succumbed to the pre-cut, cellophane-wrapped substitute for bread!), and of pouring out wine. Most of us have memories of the way father or mother presided at the table, or the way grandfather said grace. May it not have been simply the familiar gestures of Jesus that suddenly revealed to them who he was? They told "how he was known of them in breaking of bread." Whatever there was about his person in the evening light that had prevented their recognizing him as they walked, the moment they reclined around the table and he took up the bread recognition flooded in. This was indeed the Lord with whom they had lived during these eventful months. They were gripped by the familiar — and their eyes were open. In a time of anxiety and questioning they were enfolded by the vision of the Christ they had known and loved.

You will have guessed by now that this is not a "with it" sermon. I have the feeling that in the present welter of exhortations to update the Church, to streamline our worship and to change everything within reach, we may be underestimating a vital religious factor in every generation — the power of the familiar. I am not rising in defense of sheer conservatism of the type that automatically resists any change whatever in the creeds we profess, the hymns we sing, the operation of the church. A static church is a dead church. It is surely sufficient to remember that everything we treasure was new once. There was a time when the Westminster Confession was a new document. There was a time when a congregation heard "Jesus, Lover of my soul" for the first time (and half of them said: "Why can't we stick with the old hymns?"). We have to remember that those who objected to change two thousand years ago, objected to Jesus Christ.

But the swing today is to the opposite pole. On every side we are being pressed to accept changes, to update our expression of the faith, our forms of worship and our traditional activities. Some such renewal is long overdue, and as a congregation we have moved some way in this direction, yet should we not ask some serious questions about the passion for change? It would be theoretically possible for a church like this to cut loose from the past and make our expression of the faith entirely contemporary. We could eliminate everything in our worship that is not immediately understandable to anyone dropping in from the street. We could rip out from our church every symbol or decoration that is not in contemporary taste. We could use nothing but modern translations of the Bible and vernacular prayers. We could use only hymns with modern words and music. And the result would be a liturgical disaster. It is not just the older generation who would feel deprived. Everyone would feel that something vital was missing. For an absolutely essential element in real worship is the grip of the familiar. It not only conveys overtones of religious meaning that reach us in no other way but provides the rest for the mind and spirit without which true worship is impossible.

We should not allow ourselves to be bullied by the argument that we retain the familiar in deference to the sentimental attachments of the elderly. It is not only old people who respond to the power of the familiar. If you have ever read nursery tales to a child, you know how important it is that every detail must be the same as it always was, and how one story is demanded again and again in identical words. In times of trouble and stress both children and adults find refuge in the familiar. A sick child needs the presence of familiar figures and toys. A modern nation in a time of crisis — a war, an assassination, an earthquake — turns to the familiar shrines of ancestral worship. And when death comes it is very seldom that a minister is asked to arrange what you might call a "contemporary funeral service." At such a time it is the 23rd Psalm, the 14th chapter of St. John — and the King James Version — that is nearly always requested.

Why should we despise this turning to the familiar in times of turmoil? It's not only the weak and insecure that crave the familiar face in a time of danger. You find this instinct in the great heroes and leaders of the world, as well as in its saints. Think of King David — first the young man facing Goliath, rejecting the panoply of a warrior in favor of his familiar sling and stone, then later in life in a moment of acute danger, seizing the trophy of that youthful conflict, the sword of Goliath: "There is none like that: give it me." The great men of the Old Testament were sustained through turmoil and battle, through defeat and exile, by the familiar symbols of their faith, the psalms of their forefathers, and the vision of Jerusalem. "If I forget thee, O Jerusalem, let my right hand forget her cunning." The enduring strength of Judaism has lain in the grip of the familiar. And which leader of more recent times in our

69

own story — Washington, Lincoln, Churchill — has not appealed to his people with the accents of the familiar? A people in distress, a man at his wit's end, a nation in crisis does not want to hear some bright new epigram but a sustaining word with all the resonance of the well-known and trusted. And even in these days of enormously accelerated change, which of us does not still respond to this tug of the familiar?

I am aware that many come to worship today with some confusion and questioning. It may be that after some years in the wilderness you have returned to Christian worship. You are by no means prepared to renounce the spirit of free enquiry that led you to break with many of the religious traditions of your upbringing. You may even question the appeal that throbs for you in certain hymns, scriptures and ceremonies of the Church. Others who have never left the family of the Church may feel the same way. You may wonder how valid your faith really is, and how much it is just a sentimental response to the familiar. I suggest that no thinking man or woman need be afraid of the grip of the familiar. We can surely distinguish between that which is unimportant and open to the criticism of our alerted minds, and the deeper level at which God himself is communicating. We cannot worship if we are analyzing every phrase we hear, every note that is struck. But we can worship when we realize that behind and within the familiar is the beloved gesture of God. Just as

70

those disciples recognized the familiar gesture of Christ at the table; here God makes himself known as the One who summons his children in every age to the familiar contours of the Father's home. If St. Augustine was right when he said "Thou hast made us for thyself, and our hearts are restless till they rest in thee," then the grip of the familiar in our souls can be the gesture of God himself.

It is remarkable that Jesus Christ, the great innovator, the disturber of the status quo, made sure that his followers through the years ahead would be provided with something stable, enduring, unchanging and familiar. He taught them what we call the "Lord's Prayer." Even as he taught it, he warned against "vain repetitions," but he certainly knew the value of familiar words. He himself would surely repeat three times a day the familiar Shema: "Hear, O Israel, the Lord Thy God is one God." Would any of us like to dispense with the Lord's Prayer on the grounds that the words are too familiar?

Then he did more. He made sure that the recognition of his presence in the breaking of the bread would continue as long as there would be a Church on earth. "This do, in remembrance of me." When we come to Communion it is above all to recognize the presence of Christ, to relive his familiar gestures as he broke the bread and poured out the wine, speaking of his sacrificial offering for us all. Here is the most familiar rite in Christendom. Here is the gesture our fathers knew, our ancestors and the whole company of the Church in every land from the earliest days. Here, in a time of turmoil, is the grip of the familiar that steadies our faith and renews our vision. If this rite were eliminated from our liturgy in favor of something new, could you estimate the damage to our worship, the impoverishment of our faith?

If sometimes the sheer routine of certain words and actions robs them of their power, and we begin to wonder why we continue to go through the motions when the spark has gone, the answer is not to eliminate the familiar from our religion, but awaken to the Spirit of Life who makes all things new. The routine can be the pathway for his reforming power. This is why the sixteenth-century reformers reshaped, but did not destroy, the liturgy of the Church. They retained the Lord's Prayer, the creeds, Baptism, and the Holy Communion. They knew the grip of the familiar and wanted it to be known and felt again with divine and renovating power.

So we approach the Table today, invoking that same Spirit of life, and rejoicing in the grip of the familiar. This is our God who has met with each generation in the past and knows that we are not so very different in our fundamental needs. This is the Christ through whose familiar gestures at the Table we renew our vision and find ourselves welcomed "back home." And here is the Holy Spirit who makes the familiar words and symbols to glow with present meaning and enduring power. When this grip is made upon our souls, we may well want to say with those two disciples: "Did not our heart burn within us?"

7

Confidence and Compassion

And he answered, Fear not: for they that be with us are more than they that be with them.

II KINGS 6:16

Recently I asked a friend from Africa who was visiting this country for the first time in many years what his chief impression was. His answer surprised me. He said: "I come from a country where there is a lot of unrest and potential danger but we don't talk about it the way you do. What strikes me here is that everyone is shouting about the awful things that can happen in the summer or later on. It's almost as if you were all determined to talk yourselves into trouble." That was the verdict of a white man living in Malawi.

This set me thinking. I'm sure he didn't mean that we should ignore the tensions of our time, or that we should live in a fool's paradise. And I would not want to offer smooth words from the pulpit at the moment when the sober conclusions of the Kerner Report should alert every serious citizen to the extreme gravity of the racial crisis. But it did seem to me that he had put his finger on a question of morale that is very

74

much the Church's business. How can we possibly apply ourselves to the huge tasks of reshaping our cities, and unifying the nation in justice and order, in an atmosphere of either alarmed pessimism or cynical expectation of the worst?

It is one thing to be roused from our complacency and made alert to the peril we are in. It is quite another to wallow in dire prognostications, to be the impotent rumor-mongers of disaster, to nourish hopelessness and fear. We know that there is a minority among us which talks of inevitable conflict and violence and is utterly cynical about any possibilities of peaceful change or reform. They scorn any reference to the democratic process by which this nation has surmounted crises in the past. We know there is another minority who would have us meet violence with violence, and whose contribution to the situation is learning how to use a gun. But what about that silent majority of every race and color who want a land of decency and order, of expanding freedoms, and opportunity for all? Is there not still a great heartland of hope and goodwill — or is it being eroded by the forces of cynicism and fear? I am not talking about the smug apathy of those who have "never had it so good," but of the millions who still hold the Dream, who still hope for order without injustice, freedom without license, change without bloodshed. Are they losing confidence — confidence in the values of goodwill, honest debate, integrity, mutual trust, and the power of love, which are our Christian heritage? The answer to that question will determine our future more than any agitation or legislation. Recovery of confidence in such moral values is the only way to national health and hope. And that means a lively conviction that, in spite of all the horrors that stain the human landscape and test our faith, the universe is on the side of truth and honesty and tolerance and love. In other words, our confidence must have religious roots.

When confidence of this kind fails the other casualty is likely to be compassion. For the two are linked. It's only the man or woman who has this moral strength who is freed to be compassionate. The cynic cannot truly love, for he is bound by the law of the jungle he has accepted. The other day I found myself discussing the slum areas of this city with a casual travelling acquaintance. He told me he had grown up in one of them, but he had no sympathy whatever for the present inhabitants of the ghetto. "Let them make it — as I did" — that was his attitude. Similarly the panic-stricken are unable to love their neighbors in the New Testament sense, for they are afraid, and perfect fear casts out love. There's a lot of tough talk around today that pretends to be realist, but is actually hollow cynicism or disguised terror. Compassion is in danger the moment fear takes hold. Rioting and looting are not only evil in themselves but provoke a terrible backlash in which panic sets in and compassion dies. It is that kind of situation in which dictators thrive. If we are to avoid such a fate the vast reservoirs of moral strength and genuine love need to be tapped — and need to be refilled. We need a philosophy of confidence, or — if you like — a theology of hope. Whatever else religion and the churches ought to be doing at the moment they are surely called to instill this confidence in the power of goodness which is really faith in God. For only from a position of spiritual strength can true compassion flow.

So I turn to the Bible — not just because a preacher is expected to hitch his thinking to a text, but because the Bible is the mighty source-book of confidence in God and compassion for one's fellowmen. When I say "source-book" I don't mean that we find in it anything resembling the kind of polysyllabic diagnosis and recommendations that we wallow in today. The Bible may have been translated by a committee but — thank God — it wasn't written by one. It's about real people and real life. And you've got to read it with sympathy and imagination, for we are not used to its blunt ways of speaking about God and man. We've also got to learn to distinguish between the Word of God that reaches us from its heart and the words and ideas of men with which it is entangled. Thus when I speak from the Bible about confidence and compassion I don't offer you an essay on the subject but a story, a story that comes in a style, and from a context, totally different from what we are familiar with today. But it's about God and man and a time of tension; and what it says can spring to life for us today. Time has rolled on and the externals have wonderfully changed. But the internals are the same. There is always God — and man — and a time of tension.

"Fear not: for they that be with us are more than they that be with them." These words of the prophet Elisha are to be heard in context. Taken alone they could make a dangerous text. I suppose all of us are tempted to get into the "numbers game" in defense of what we hold dear. We comfort ourselves with the statistic showing that the majority of citizens in the U.S.A. are church members. So we think the forces of decency and order are bound to prevail over license and crime. Or we estimate the arsenal of the democracies and reckon that we may have the edge over all possible enemies. There are those who have to make these calculations, but it is emphatically not this kind of confidence of which the Bible speaks. "Woe unto them," says Isaiah, ". . . that trust in chariots, because they are many; and in horsemen, because they are very strong; but they look not unto the Holy One of Israel, neither seek the Lord!" "They that be with us are more than they that be with them," is not just a variant of Voltaire's satirical remark that God is always on the side of the big battalions. Elisha here is speaking for the people of God, for those who are alarmed by the power of wickedness and begin to doubt whether goodness and justice and compassion are more than flickering lights doomed to extinction in a merciless universe. There are times when we feel encircled by a harsh and hostile world that is utterly indifferent to the values we have been taught to cherish. It is then that we need to hear this word and to realize the invisible resources of the Spirit. We then know what is meant by the saying that one man, one woman, *with God*, is always in a majority.

Elisha and his young companion were indeed surrounded. The Syrian king, having learned that the secret weapon of the Israelites was the intelligence service provided by the prophet Elisha, had sent a powerful force to trap him. So when the youth woke in the early morning he found that the surrounding hills were alive with armed men and chariots and spears glittering in the rising sun. His heart sank and he rushed to bring the news to the prophet: "Alas, my master, what shall we do?" Then came the answer: "Fear not: for they that be with us are more than they that be with them." That must have seemed as absurd to him as similar words would have been spoken by Dietrich Bonhoeffer to a fellow-prisoner in a Gestapo cell. But what followed? "Elisha prayed, and said, Lord, I pray thee, open his eyes, that he may see. And the Lord opened the eyes of the young man; and he saw:

and, behold, the mountain was full of horses and chariots of fire round about Elisha."

Do we really need to ask what kind of a vision this was? Every man or woman who has stood by what is right "though the heavens fall;" everyone who has had the courage to act in love when hatred was the order of the day; everyone who has sweetened a time of tension with confidence and compassion has seen these horses and chariots of fire. Socrates saw them when he preferred death to denying the truth his conscience perceived. Daniel saw them in the lion's den. Christians are seeing them today in the martyred churches where all human power is against them. And don't you think they were there in the dream of Martin Luther King? Here is the confidence that, though the powers of evil and the absurd are massed around us, the universe is lit by an ultimate Goodness whose instruments of love surround us and are visible to the eye of faith. It is as if, when we are disheartened and discouraged, the saints and martyrs are praying like Elisha: "Lord, I pray thee open his eyes." For they are the ones who, as was said of Moses, "endured as seeing him who is invisible."

The Christian cannot help remembering the supreme demonstration of confidence and faith in the Lord he worships. For Jesus the "horses and chariots of fire" were so real that he could openly reject the thought of their physical intervention to save his life. "Thinkest thou that I cannot now pray to my Father, and he will presently give me more than twelve legions of angels?" That was exactly what they taunted him for not doing. "If thou be the Son of God, come down from the cross." But he did not come down. He "endured as seeing him who is invisible, and died in the confidence that, even through that terrible moment, "they that be with us are more than they that be with them." And since today we worship him, risen from the dead, we know how true this is. To live in the Easter light is to be persuaded that God is in control and that "neither death nor life, nor angels, nor principalities, nor powers, nor things present, nor things to come, nor height, nor depth, nor any other creature, shall be able to separate us from the love of God which is in Christ Jesus our Lord."

How do we know that this is not a spurious confidence? Could this vision of the horses and chariots of fire not be an illusion? There is no way of proving intellectually that it is not an illusion, nor can it be proved that any human conviction is not an illusion. A man's cynicism can be an illusion; his materialism can be an illusion, or his atheism, agnosticism, or any theory of life. The point is that we all, unless we are mere cabbages, must live by faith. And this is the faith we choose when once we have been exposed to the Word of the Bible and the challenge of the Christ. We take our stand with those whose inner eyes have been opened to the "horses and chariots of fire," who are persuaded that, in the end, it is love and goodness and justice and truth that are invincible and eternally alive.

Such confidence, however, is only genuine if it issues in compassion. That is the test. Mere mystic assurance of God's goodness that inspires no reflection of his love in our daily life is not what the Bible teaches. Look at the fascinating movement of this story from the Book of Kings. The immediate result of Elisha's confidence and prayer seems at first sight to be a typical piece of oriental fantasy and revenge. For in answer to his prayer, we are told, the enemy is stricken with blindness. And Elisha cunningly pretends to lead them where they want to go, whereas in fact he delivers them helpless into the hands of the King of Israel in his capital of Samaria. That doesn't sound like a very edifying consequence of his magnificent vision. But what follows? The King of Israel is overjoyed as he watches his enemies herded like cattle before him. We can see him rubbing his hands and gloating as he turns to the prophet. "My father, shall I smite them? Shall I smite them?" If the story ended there I would not have chosen it to illustrate our theme. But it doesn't.

"He answered, Thou shalt not smite them: wouldest thou smite those whom thou hast taken captive with thy sword and with thy bow? Set bread and water

82

before them, that they may eat and drink, and go to their master." This is one of the most moving passages in the Old Testament. For we have to remember that, by the rules of the game, men taken like this were normally slaughtered without mercy. And here is Elisha, their enemy directing that they should be treated with hospitality and compassion and sent home. "He prepared great provision for them: and when they had eaten and drunk, he sent them away, and they went to their master. So the bands of Syria came no more into the land of Israel."

It is such flashes of divine compassion that illuminate the cruel pages of so much Old Testament history and show how the vision of God was leading men onwards to higher paths. I want you to note how it was Elisha's immense confidence in God that set him free from the savage customs of his day, and let him act in compassion. This is the magnanimous gesture of the man who is not afraid.

The Christian contribution to a time of tension must surely mean both the confidence that sees the invisible "chariots of fire," and the compassion that liberates the prisoners. We don't come here for a vision that provokes no action for the liberation of our fellowmen. Nor can we plunge into such action effectively unless we are girded with the confidence that the vision inspires. The choice before the Church today is not between the vision and the action. We must have

83

both. The poet William Blake was a visionary and mystic to an unusual degree. But he was consumed by a desire to help to liberate the captives of the English industrial revolution, the slum dwellers of his day. That's why we are still moved by his words:

"Bring me my bow of burning gold!
Bring me my arrows of desire!
Bring me my spear! O clouds unfold!
Bring me my chariot of fire!

I will not cease from mental fight,
Nor shall my sword sleep in my hand,
Till we have built Jerusalem,
In England's green and pleasant land."

There's fear in our world; and cynicism, violence, and oppression. If we are to be the people of compassion, if we are to play a part, however small, in bridging the divisions, and healing the hurts, we must act in the confidence that there is immense spiritual strength to be drawn on, for "they that be with us are more than they that be with them." This is no counting of heads. It is the basic belief that God in Christ is still at work through the tensions of our time "reconciling the world unto himself." This is the truth that burns in our worship. And this is the truth that sets us free.

84

8

How Can We Believe in a God of Love?

There be many that say, Who will shew us any good? Lord, lift thou up the light of thy countenance upon us.

PSALM 4:6

The psalmist might have been listening as we lay down the morning newspaper after skimming the headlines, or as TV sets are switched off after the 11 P.M. newscast. "Who will show us any good?" The wounded are carried to the helicopter, a village goes up in flames — is that good? Someone is screaming in angry protest and mobs are showing their teeth — is that good? A train is derailed and the coaches are piled up like matchwood above broken bodies — is that good? Refugees stagger across bridges with the remnants of their homes in their hands — is that good? An earthquake swallows up a village and leaves a trail of havoc and horror in its wake — is that good? The psalmist can say it again now that we have instruments beyond his dreams for showing us what is going on in the world: "There be many that say, Who will show us any good?"

Well, who? The preacher? He's surely the one whose

job it is to show something good, to point to the light in the darkness. He's the dealer in comfort, the expert in silver linings, the man with the stock of cheerful little stories, happiness pills to be swallowed once weekly after breakfast. "Who will show us any good?" they asked, and the answer was: "The preacher." So they came knocking on the psalmist's door. But it didn't open at that moment. He was not standing there with a pile of ready-made answers to their questions. He was in the inner chamber with the door closed, talking to his Father in secret. Outside the question was sighing through the streets and battering at the door: "Who will show us any good?" And inside there was a man on his knees: "Lord, lift thou up the light of thy countenance upon us."

Nowhere in the Bible is psalmist, or prophet, or preacher, or priest depicted as the man with a set of snappy answers to the agonizing questions of human life. In fact the ones who tried to divert attention from the facts by offering "something good" were labeled false prophets, phony preachers. The psalmist and the preacher have two good reasons for not offering a quick, pre-fabricated answer to the despairing cry: "Who will show us any good?" In the first place, they are not free to indulge in any cynical or stoical attitudes. They can't say: "Well, that's life, brother," or "There's good and bad, you know, and it will all be the same in a thousand years," or "The stars are against

us now, but our luck will change." They are committed to the belief that our lives are in the hands of
God, and that this God is a God of love. So the question takes the acute form: "Who will show us how a
God of love can let this happen, or this, or this ... ?"
And there are no smooth arguments to be given in
reply. In the second place the psalmist knows, as the
preacher should know, that he occupies no middle
ground between God and man. He is not up there with
chunks of infallible wisdom in his hands, ready to show
all comers what is good. He knows he has to sweat it
out with everyone else. So his answer is not an argument but a prayer — a *common* prayer: "Lord, lift
thou up the light of thy countenance upon us."

It is in this mood that I ask the question: How can
we believe in a God of love? It is a very old question
— at least as old as the Book of Job, whose author
struggled for an answer with as much passion of spirit
and integrity of mind as any modern. He shows us a
man who can find no good in the evils that have
rained upon him, and no sign of a God of justice —
let alone love. "Oh, that I knew where I might find
him! ... I would order my cause before him, and fill
my mouth with arguments." Nothing new has been
added to the problem since that book was written. Yet
the question is somehow always new. It is as new as
the disaster that happened yesterday, the agony that
kept a man awake last night. It's new when it hits us,

personally, today. That's why the psalmist didn't open the door and quote from the law and the prophets. And that's why I could not reach into the accumulated sermons of twenty-two years to pluck out the answers I have tried to give a hundred times to this same question.

Yet perhaps the very best place to start thinking about this question is in the solidarity of the human race. It's not just your question, or my question. Of course it comes at us at special times with peculiar force, but the problem is there all the time, everywhere. Isn't it strange how when some terrible calamity comes our way we are apt to say: "How can God allow this to happen?" as if this were really the first time the question had been seriously raised? We don't stop to think that when the world seemed a very good place to us, for somebody else the darkness had closed in. We are tempted to question the goodness of God when an accident happens in our street, but the news of a flood in China where millions are drowned may leave us unmoved. We think it a terrible indictment of the God of love that we should be exposed to annihilation by a bomb, but we pass over the fearful predicament of millions in other places and at other times who have been exposed to mutilation and extermination on a fearful scale. We need to let history and common sense teach us, gently but firmly, that this is a human problem, a constant problem, one that does not emerge simply when the dark side of life swoops down on *us*. We face this together as a human family. In view of the precariousness of life, the injustice and the cruelty, the random distribution of suffering, how can *we* believe in a God of love?

It may be that the question became more acute for this generation that has seen the slaughter of two world wars and the horror of the concentration camps. But in the end is it the sheer quantity of suffering that raises the problem? If we are truly sensitive to goodness and justice, if we are in this together, then one child dying in India through malnutrition challenges the reality of the love of God as much as Belsen or Hiroshima.

So the question is universal and unchanging. And it is not alleviated by the pious observation that what seems contrary to our ideas of justice and love is the result of human sin. Sure, wars and crimes are the result of human sin, but can we say that the victims are the guilty? And what about floods, and famines, and earthquakes? Whose sin made the earth to quake and gape and swallow a child?

"Who will show us any good?" I take you right down to the depths, to dark mystery that is beyond all understanding — not because this is the whole truth about life, but because it is there more than anywhere else that the God of love takes hold of us and there, incredibly, that he lifts up the light of his countenance upon us. The older I grow the more clearly I see that belief in the God of love grows out of our experience in the valley where everything seems to deny it. How wrong the skeptic can be when he imagines that we cling to our trust in the Father-God by shutting our eyes to the injustice and the suffering, and dwelling on the joys of the Father's world where,

> "All nature sings, and round me rings
> The music of the spheres."

And how wrong the Christian apologist can be when he tries to argue that the balance of the evidence points conclusively to the absolute control of a God of perfect love. It doesn't. The most sheer argument can do is to reveal that, in the end, we must make our choice — and take the consequences. Either there is no meaning, no pattern, and no God behind all this; or there is a good God struggling forever against an unconquerable darkness; or there is a dark God who sports with us for a few years before oblivion; or there is a God of total and consuming love whose plans, like his peace, pass all our understanding. Whatever you decide to believe, you make an act of faith; and, as you believe, so in the end you will live — for the light of the countenance of the God, the devil, or the non-God you choose will in the end be reflected in the depths of your soul.

The poet has seen very well that the God of love is not an axiom of the mind, a cold cliché lodged in the creeds of the Church, but the Hound of Heaven

who tracks us down "through the labyrinthine ways ...
and in the mist of tears ... and under running laugh-
ter." We believe in him, not because, like Dr. Pangloss,
we see "that all is for the best in the best of all
possible worlds," but because in the ambiguities of this
mortal life he will not let us go. Like Job we find that
when we want to scream our protests to the empty
heavens we discover that they are not empty — and we
are talking to our God. Like Paul, when our best
prayers seem to have bounced back from the stony
vault of the unseen, we hear the whisper: "My grace
is sufficient for thee." Like George Matheson, the
hymn writer, stricken with blindness, depressed by his
labors in a dull and unresponsive Edinburgh church,
we too have known the compulsive cry: "O Love that
wilt not let me go."

We believe in the God of love because this is the
God who meets us in the darkness. And when, as
sometimes happens, he seems to have forsaken us and
there is no echo of his presence, to whom do we turn?
Would you really want to join the ranks of those who
say: "Who will show us any good?" the company of
the cynics who invite us to empty our religious beliefs
into the trash can, or of the skeptics whose faith is
frozen in the chilly suspense of the mind and will?
Would you not rather go, as I would, to the communion of the saints, to the men and women of every
age who have known what it is to kneel in the darkness

and pray: "Lord, lift thou up the light of thy countenance upon us"? The saint is not the one congealed in the dim devotion of a stained-glass window, or dwelling in some distant monastery. The saint is the man or woman we know who makes it easier for us to believe in the God of love. And the communion of saints, in which we profess to believe, is nothing other than the surrounding of our own doubting and despairing selves by the circle of light that is reflected in the faces of those who live in the love of God.

But suppose, you may say, that the worst should happen. Suppose the powers of evil should have full rein. Suppose that wickedness, injustice, corruption, violence, should run amok and smother the company of the saints. Suppose a saint should appear in whom the love of God was perfectly reflected here on earth, and be totally unable to protect himself from the hate and fury of the demonic forces that are loose among men. Suppose a day when no one can "show us any good," when the sky is darkened, the earth quakes, and this good man dies without a flicker of comfort from the God of love. What then? Could we any longer believe in him?

It happened, you know. All this happened. The Church is here today to remind us that it happened. Every single argument that we could use to deny the reality and presence of a God of love blazes from the Cross of Calvary. The Innocent suffers — what an Innocent, and what suffering! Wickedness runs riot without a sign from heaven. The courage of decent men is sapped, while the brutality of the crowd is reinforced. The hands that healed are pierced with nails. The eyes that were lifted to the Father are clouded with the pain of utter desolation. The tongue that blessed is swollen in fearful thirst. The darkness that descends blots out all meaning, and mocks the words about the God of love "without whom no sparrow falls to the ground." Where is he now? "Who will show us any good" in this terrible scene?

But this, miraculously, is exactly where Christians find their God of love. For we believe that this was not a meaningless spectacle played out in a grim and godless arena. "God was in Christ reconciling the world unto himself." The God of love was not absent, but present in the very heart of the horror, for in Jesus Christ he was giving, giving, giving himself, so that after this there need be no fear, there need be no despair, there need be no doubt that his love will work in *all* things for good with them that love him. Here is the proof of God's love for us, said St. Paul. No argument for the mind; no sentimental appeal. Just this: "While we were yet sinners Christ died for us."

The cry is still sounding in the streets: "Who will show us any good?" We live with it, and we hear its echo in our souls. But we come here to join the psalmist and the saint, to find the answer on our knees.

"Lord, lift thou up the light of thy countenance upon us." In a world where not only man but nature itself is infected with evil we live by this light, the light that burned through the darkness when Christ died, and blazes now in his resurrection power. So we go back to the daily newspaper, back to the light and shade of our homes and jobs, back to the tasks that sometimes daunt us, back to the ideals that have been threatened and the goals that have lost their allure, confident that the light is still there, and that nothing — in earth or heaven or hell, "can separate us from the love of God, which is in Christ Jesus our Lord."

9

Cool Christianity

*And they told him, that Jesus of Nazareth passeth by.
And he cried, saying, Jesus, thou Son of David, have
mercy on me.* ST. LUKE 18:37, 38

Notice the highlights in this story. Jesus of Nazareth
was passing by. The blind beggar cried out for help.
Jesus asked: "What do you want me to do for you?"
He replied: "To receive my sight." And Jesus said:
"Receive your sight; your faith has saved you," and
healed him.

You may say: "A familiar story; there are many like
it in the Gospels." Yes, but we may easily miss the
curious contrast between this picture and the one so
many of us have in the back of the mind. We think of
Jesus as the preacher and healer who sought people
out to help them. Our version of this story would then
read: "Jesus of Nazareth looked for the blind beggar,
went up to him, and said: 'Can I help you?'." But this
is *not* what happened. There is almost what you might
call a cool, casual note in the story. Jesus was passing
by. He was interrupted by the beggar's cry. And then
he asked what must have seemed an utterly superfluous
question: "What do you want of me?" Finally, we are
told that it was the beggar's own faith that healed him.

95

And Jesus went on his way.

The more I think about this story, and the others like it in the Gospels, the more I question some of our assumptions about Christianity in action. For haven't we been trained to think of the Gospel as an offer of help to men and women, God's approach to us with divine assistance? And isn't the popular idea of the Church that of a community commissioned to press this Gospel on the world? Don't we think of our task as a congregation, and as individual Christians, to go where the need is, saying: "Can I help you?" Doesn't the very idea of "mission" suggest reaching out for people, offering help, bringing them something they need? Yet this story, and the whole tenor of the Gospels, could make us wonder if we've got it wrong. When you begin to think about it, is there any recorded instance of Christ approaching anyone with his offer of help? We find him sought out by people like Nicodemus, by a Roman centurion, by Mary Magdalene, by the Syro-Phoenician woman, by the woman stretching out her hands in the crowd and by a host of others. But can you think of any instance where he took the lead, intruding himself with an offer of help? He certainly sent his disciples out on a mission, but didn't he warn them not to intrude? If they were not wanted they were to get out. And didn't he utter a scathing condemnation of proselytism? "Woe unto you!" he said to the religious leaders of his day, "for ye compass sea and land to make one proselyte, and when he is made ye make him twofold more the child of hell than yourselves." If this is mission, it's cool, not hot.

Now in case someone is thinking: "Wonderful! I always did think religion is a private affair and that we should never talk about it to anyone else. I always did resent being told that I ought to be much more active in the outreach of the church. I always did question this business of missions, either at home or abroad," I want to make some things perfectly clear.

Christianity is not a private possession of any one of us. From the beginning it has been a mission, and it will always be so. You and I are the long-range products of a Christian mission, for our religion was not founded in America or in Europe. And the Gospel is an offer of help, help we receive from God, and help we are bound to offer to others. The Church's role most certainly *is* to help wherever there is human need. I believe in mission, in the contagion of the faith, in the necessity of Christian action. I believe that a church that ceases to be a mission ceases to be a church. I believe that no one can truly know Christ without longing for others to know him too. I believe that it is the authentic voice of Chist that still calls to us. "Go ye therefore, and teach all nations, baptizing them in the name of the Father, and of the Son, and of the Holy Ghost."

The question is not: "Does God, does Christ really

offer help?" "Should the Church, should I, offer help?"
The question is *"How?"*

Let's take this question: "Can I help you?" There's
more than one way of saying it. This summer I found
myself one day in Lisbon trying to make myself understood to a ticket agent who spoke only Portuguese. Just
when negotiations seemed hopelessly stalled, I heard
a sweet voice behind me, saying in perfect English:
"Can I help you?" I turned round, and there was a
very charming nun who spoke both English and Portuguese and was there just when I needed help. So my
problems at the ticket office were swiftly solved. (As a
result of this encounter an ecumenical dialogue developed which ended with my escorting one of her
colleagues to Oporto — but that's another story.) There
are moments in life when: "Can I help you?" sounds
like music in the ear. We want some competent help to
extricate us from a desperate situation, and the "can-
I-help-you" person comes like an angel of mercy.

But I'm sure you will agree that there are other times
when this offer of help is an intrusion and a nuisance.
There's a way of saying: "Can I help you" that implies
something like: "You look a helpless sort of person, and
I'm just the one to solve your problems." It can even
imply: "For goodness' sake stop hanging around, make
up your mind and get out of my way!" Sometimes it
even suggests: "You're a suspicious-looking character and
the help you need is probably the police!" If, like me,

you enjoy browsing round a bookstore, you don't want to hear this question. Nor do we when we are wandering round a museum, thinking our own thoughts or just idling in some public place. At such times our instinctive answer to the offer of help is: "Go away and leave me alone."

There's a question of *intrusion* here that we need to think about when considering the Christian mission. The desire to help or to communicate our faith to someone else, does not imply a rough invasion of privacy, a lack of respect for the other's right to be left alone. Christianity is not a kind of patent medicine that God has given us to press on other people without regard to their feelings or convictions. According to Christ's commands, we are to be there, ready to help where men and women are hungry, despairing, hopeless: we are to be alert to the need — sensitive and outgoing. But we must respect that inner citadel where another has the right to be alone. It is one of the most remarkable features of the Gospels that in their records Christ never intrudes on anyone. Again and again, he waits to be asked. But then he never fails to respond. In the whole reach of the Bible picture of God what is more amazing than his infinite patience and respect for the personality of each one of his straying human family. He comes to meet us in our need, yes, but always awaiting our movement towards him. That's why there is such a thing as prayer. And how did he make his most powerful offer of help to man? By a spectacular invasion of the human scene, sending in his spiritual tanks to bring a deliverance that no one asked for? No; by letting his Son be born in a stable, and allowing mankind to do with as they pleased. The Cross reveals that God's great "Can I help you?" awaits our response — for it is the intrusion that is not an intrusion, the intrusion of love. And what I mean by "Cool Christianity" is the loving concern that prays, that is there, that is ready to act — but never intrudes.

Then there's the question of *competence.* Sometimes when we, as individuals or the Church offer our help, someone should call our bluff. In the play "Harvey" some years ago, which was about an alcoholic who believed he was followed around by a large rabbit with that name, I seem to remember his delightful answer to the many friends who offered their help. "Just what exactly did you have in mind?" Such a reply punctures the vague pretensions of many "Can-I-help-you's?" This applies not only to our futile gestures of assistance that we often make more to pacify our conscience than with any real help in mind, but also to the current tendency of the Christian Church to invade every section of life with comments and advice.

It is, of course, the duty of the Church to speak in the name of Christian principle in public affairs. But that is very different from assuming an authority in every field, and issuing pronouncements on topics where we have no special competence. If a churchman were to approach a politician and ask: "Can I help you?", I can imagine that the reply might be: "Yes; you can help me see the moral implications of certain controversies; you can help me practice my faith in the tangled and testing business of politics; you can help me remember my God and my duty to my neighbor — but if you mean: 'Can I do your job for you?' my answer is 'No! Leave me alone!'" A cooler Christianity would not press upon the state so many of its opinions in matters more technical than moral.

Then, there is the fearful question of *superiority*. While the Christian must be ready to help when he can, at the right time and place, there is a certain arrogance in the "Can-I-help-you?" attitude when it implies that we are always able to reach down from our superior position. Being genuinely ready to help is something different from assuming that we are always able to supply just what another man or woman needs. It is one thing to be a faithful witness to Christ and tell another about our experience of him: it is quite another to try to impose our views on another with no respect whatever for his own convictions. We may be persuaded that Christ is the Savior of all men, and the supreme revelation of God, but that by no means implies that we have any kind of moral superiority over the one who professes another faith — or none at all.

The more we think about it the more complex this business of offering help becomes. If we have ever been on the receiving end, we must know that it is not always a joyful experience. Sometimes it can be shattering and humiliating. Hence the need for the utmost humility and self-effacement on the part of the one who offers help. We are learning, for instance, that when we approach the ghettos of poverty with any kind of superior: "Can-I-help-you?" attitude, we are sure to be rebuffed. We know that help is needed — and conversely, that we need help in understanding this situation — but our manner must never be what the French call "de haut en bas." I remember my English mother-in-law once telling me how as a young lady in London she had gone "slumming" — as it used to be called. As the door of a squalid apartment opened and she began to explain how she wanted to help, she was met with the retort: "Go away! Don't come here saving your soul on me!" Cool Christianity avoids this patronizing attitude and avoids the pitfalls of pride and self-service. That is why so much true Christian giving is quiet and anonymous.

The Book of Job gives us a dramatic example of the rejection of the wrong kind of help. Here is a man in the depths of disaster and despair, and soon the so-called "comforters" gather round him like vultures. "Can I help you?" And Job listens to what they have to say, to their glib explanations of his misfortunes, to their religious platitudes, to their superior tone of voice. Then he rounds on them. "No doubt but ye are the people, and wisdom shall die with you." "I have heard many such things: miserable comforters are ye all."

"Jesus of Nazareth passeth by." "Passeth by" — there is no intrusion, no pushing in, no arrogance, no air of superiority. Think who this was: the Son of God who came "to seek and to save that which was lost," the One who had every competence to help, inexhaustible resources of divine love and healing. He comes within reach, but he doesn't intrude. It is the beggar who cries out to him. And even then he doesn't immediately offer the healing power. "What do you want me to do?" An extraordinary question in the circumstances — yet time and again we find that he waits for a man or woman to put their needs into words. Then, when the healing happens, what does he say? "*Thy* faith hath saved thee." What an extraordinary reverence and respect for the human personality shines through the whole story.

Cool Christianity — the Bible tells of a God, of a Savior, who is most able to help us, One whose grace we need more than anything else, who nevertheless patiently waits for us to ask. That's why the Bible is so full of prayers. For prayer is our way of responding when God's grace is near, when "Jesus of Nazareth passeth by." This patience of God is devastating — for how terribly possible it is for us to miss the help, to refuse the grace. We have a built-in tendency to ignore this patient God, to remain in our blindness when the Healer passes by. "Adam, where art thou?" "Leave me alone." "Cain, where is thy brother Abel?" "Leave me alone." It is the guilt in us that prompts this response. For the One who offers help is the God of infinite love and understanding, yet we think we are better on our own. Even when that Love is poured into a human life in the supreme appeal to mankind, it does not come with the intrusive and commanding power of a divine dictator. It is incarnate in a child born in a stable, in a man with no place to lay his head, in a victim of our sins nailed on a cross. And "Jesus of Nazareth passeth by." He still passes, and still waits for our response, in our own words, with our own faith.

If we have made that response, if in any way we have known what it is to have our eyes opened, our sins forgiven, our life empowered, then we naturally long to make this Christ known to others. But we must do it in his way — with infinite respect and humble patience. There are times when we have to declare what we believe, just as the Church is charged to make known the Gospel. But along with the sincere and humble witness of the lips goes the silent demonstration of a life. The person we turn to in trouble is not always the one who is there saying: "Can I help you?", but the one in whom we have come to find a reflection of the Christ. For we know that here is no superiority or pride of soul, but patience, understanding, generosity and the help we really need.

This is the "Cool Christianity" I am talking about. It's not a tepid, careless, take-it-or-leave-it attitude to the Gospel, but a calm, trusting, patient, yet passionately caring demonstration of Christian living. If those who think that Christianity is a busy, interfering, pushy religion would read the Gospels and consider Christ; if they would turn from the strident and arrogant distortions of the faith that stain the Christian record, to the witness of the real saints, ancient and modern, in every section of the Church, then they might hear the voice of him who knows exactly what we need and waits patiently to bestow it. "Jesus of Nazareth passeth by." It is for us who have cried out for his help to be likewise present, without intruding, where the need is greatest in the world we know.

10

Our Confidence in Christ

He said to them, 'Why are you such cowards? Have you no faith even now?' They were awestruck and said to one another, 'Who can this be whcm even the wind and the sea obey?'

ST. MARK 4:40, 41 (NEB)

Who can this be who calls us cowards because we are afraid of the storm? Who can this be who seems to be asleep at the moment of danger? Who can this be who speaks the word of power so that the wind drops and there is a dead calm? Read on, and you find him among the tombstones where there was a raving lunatic with hell raging inside him, and again the word is spoken and there is a dead calm. Read on, and you are with a father whose little daughter is dying, with a woman suffering twelve years with hemorrhages. Who can this be who walks into the dark center of the human storm and out again leaving a peace that passes all understanding?

I am not here to tell you who he is. The Church has its venerable statements about Jesus Christ, but no one here will brandish them under your nose and say: "Sign on the dotted line, and you can be one of us." We try to stand aside and let him make his own impression. How differently men and women responded when they

106

met him in Galilee and Jerusalem. "Is not this the carpenter, the son of Mary?" "What wisdom is this that has been given him?" "I am not worthy to have you come under my roof." "You are the Christ, the Son of the living God!" and — from the same man — "Depart from me, for I am a sinful man, O Lord;" "Lord remember me!" Who can this be of whom these two things are said — "A gluttonous man and a winebibber," and "My Lord and my God"?

Who can this be? Men have never stopped asking the question — and still in the present tense. The artists have responded and each one seems to see a different Christ. The novelists, the dramatists and the moviemakers have responded — and not one satisfies you or me that this is the Christ we know. Yet no one can say that the image of Christ has faded into the mists of a million interpretations. He looms upon this generation with an undiminished charisma and a power to change the lives of men. He is not lost in the shadows of history. Even now, a poem is being written in some language that speaks of Christ; a glittering window is erected in which he glows in the colors of today; in an attic in Greenwich Village a girl fashions her vision of Christ in clay; a broken life is being mended by something called his "grace;" and food is being flown into Biafra impelled by his Spirit.

We here have been answering the question: "Who can this be?" in as many different ways as there are people present. But the reason we are here is that there is a real Christ and he has drawn us. The reason we are united in a church is that there is one Lord. Nothing else can identify us in this seething city. We share with hundreds of other groups a concern for social justice, for freedom, for world peace; but if we have no plus to bring, no compelling vision, no faith that reaches beyond our human limits, no confidence that there is a mighty Spirit on the side of the good for which we struggle, then why be a church? Christ is that plus, that vision, that faith, that Spirit. When we seek "the crux of the matter", as the word suggests, we find a Cross. The storms of our world converge on the Man we see there, and we ask again, "Who can this be?"

I bring you this storm scene from the Lake of Galilee because it raises the crucial question of our confidence in Christ. It is not comfortable to hear this voice: "Why are you such cowards? Have you no faith even now?" We want to answer: "But I'm willing to stand up and be counted on the Christian side, and I *do* have faith — otherwise I wouldn't be here." But there's another side to the story, isn't there? Is there anyone here who has not known the fear that clutches when the plane drops a thousand feet, and I don't mean that just literally (stomach-heaving though it is). I mean that sudden drop when the bottom falls out of life and what we relied on isn't there any more. And what about these moments when the sheer weight of what we hear about slums and war, and crime and hideous cruelties makes us cry out: "God, it isn't worth the struggle — the sum total of goodwill in our world is like a flickering candle in a high wind."? When we drop the blinkers we may wear in church and take a hard look at the way of the world, don't we secretly agree at times with the remark made at our discussion group last Sunday: "It's a losing battle we are in."? And then there is the ultimate fear that hovers over this generation and seeps through our thin protective layer of faith — that there is no point to it all, that when everything dissolves this little planet will go on spinning through the emptiness as if there had never been a human family at all. How strong, I want to ask in all frankness, how strong really is our faith in God, our confidence in Christ?

"Have you no faith even now?" This, more than anything else is the kind of man this is — the man who asks for faith, faith in the God who lives in him. Once they overheard him say in a kind of wistful aside: "When the Son of Man comes will he find faith on earth?" The spiritual power the churches need, the spiritual renewal so many of us are seeking, is not a diversion from our concern with the city we live in, and the seething problems of a divided world. The faith that develops in a spiritual hothouse remote from the traffic of contemporary life is not Christian faith. There is no iron curtain hung between our meetings on Tuesday and Thursday with their emphasis on the practical and immediate problems, the formation of task forces and what we are doing now. The crux of the matter is the kind of confidence in Christ that sends us out into the storm. That is the living faith he calls for — that which impels us to meet the challenge, not that which offers us a way to escape it.

There are times when I wish we could tear up the whole dictionary of conventional religion and start afresh with new words and new images to express what confidence in Christ can do for a man or woman who lives in the real word. For the phrases we use are the tired blood of the ecclesiastical body. Their vitality has gone, and the Gospel hovers around like the ghost of a former piety, instead of being, as Jesus said, *"life,* and life more abundant." But — thank God — he can break through in every generation and communicate directly in ways beyond our understanding. We need more than ears that pass ideas to the brain. We need the inward eye that catches the vision, the spirit that responds to the tug of the unseen, the readiness to let go the little bit of religion that may be standing in the way of Christ.

So today we meet him in the storm. He was there with the disciples where the wind came lashing down and the little boats were rocking in the gale. He is still in the storm. When we say "Christ" today so many have an image of a remote and cloudy figure to be sought in the shadows of the sanctuary. Was I wrong in thinking that for some the display of pictures last week in our Parish Hall was vaguely "irreligious"? These grubby children in the slum to which the text was fixed: "Of such is the Kingdom of God"? This rubbing of our noses in the realities of war, starvation, disease and racial hatreds? Who would not rather have soft lights, soothing music and a bright picture of a handsome Christ surrounded by scrubbed and happy boys and girls? Is that what you think? Do you want to find him in a holy corner where you can forget the beastliness we read of every day? I don't blame those who say: "I don't come to church to get another dose of the horrors I can see on TV or the worries that the commentators force upon me." Too much modern religion is just holding up a magnifying glass to the messy world. We have something else to say. But, if we are looking for Christ *this is where we begin.*

He is in the storm. That's why I have confidence in him. The Son of God was born in a slum; he mixed with the physically, mentally and morally diseased, and he died a squalid and horrible death. There's nothing that revolts us in our world, nothing that makes us heartsick and afraid that he did not know — right down to the edge of that black pit where God seems to have forsaken us. He's been through it — that's why I trust him. Have you ever felt almost immediately drawn to someone you casually meet without quite knowing why? Then you discover that there has been a shared

111

experience. You've both been there. So you trust one another. It's as simple as that.

Now listen to this scream from the throats of frightened men: "Master, we are sinking! Do you not care?" (One of the reasons why I accept this story factually is that I can't imagine an apostle inventing this shaming moment of panic.) "Do you not care?" It was a vote of no confidence at the moment of despair. We now really are at the crux of the matter. Honestly, do you deeply believe that God really cares? Have you that sort of confidence when things go wrong, when you watch the way the world goes lurching from crisis to crisis, when you think of the victims of war, drugs or muggings in the street? How can I tell you to have confidence in Christ? What is he doing about it?

The question is not answered by a verbal assurance from the pulpit. It's not enough for me to tell you that Christ is with us in the storm. You must find him there yourself. And how do we find him? Surely only as we ask the other question: "Do I care?" We don't gain confidence in Christ by simply crying for refuge "when the nearer waters roll, when the tempest still is high." We've got to care about those for whom the waters are rolling nearer than to us, and whose tempest is worse than ours. That's why we have been trying to see our way forward as a church that cares; cares about conditions in this city, cares about people in every corner of the world whatever label they wear. Did anyone say this more powerfully than Christ himself? It is the merciful who will receive mercy; the forgiving who will be forgiven; the caring who will know the caring of our God. "Lord, when saw we thee hungry and fed thee? or thirsty and gave thee drink? When saw we thee a stranger, and took thee in? or naked, and clothed thee?" "And the King shall answer and say unto them: Verily I say unto you, Inasmuch as ye have done it unto one of the least of these my brethren, ye have done it unto me."

Does it matter how feeble our efforts seem, how puny the works of mercy over against the great tide of evil? The faith of those who are engaged in the struggle whether they are Christians or not is that they will go on caring though the heavens fall. The Christian knows that the heavens will not fall for in his caring he meets — sometimes without even knowing it — the vast caring of God. For Christ is there in that act of mercy. Christ is there in the middle of the storm. And we have confidence in him.

Much that I read today in the literature of the Church is content to leave the matter there — Christ in the storm; Christ the "man for others." But I must let the whole story speak. And there is more. "The wind dropped and there was a dead calm." "Who can this be whom even the wind and the sea obey?" There is something here that cannot be talked away by futile discussion about miracles or ignored by a church that wants to be true to the New Testament. Whatever the sequence of events that day on the Sea of Galilee, Christ comes to us in this story as the one who was not only *in* the storm: he was beyond it. I cannot express my confidence in Christ in purely humanistic terms. "Who is this whom even the wind and the sea obey?" It is the same one who drove the devils from the possessed, who spoke a word of forgiveness that made a prostitute a saint, who claimed a Kingdom "not of this world," and who returned from death and hell to give his disciples a confidence that turned the world upside-down. I have confidence in Christ because from him there flows the spiritual power of one who is above the storm. I have confidence in Christ because he makes himself known as the one who triumphs over death, and one to whom the whole creation moves.

These are big statements — for some, meaningless statements. Yet this would not be a Christian Church unless here we could meet the one beyond the storm. We might astonish one another if one day we dropped all shyness and told each other how we had met him. I don't mean a bouquet of "success stories" — for which of us has not known the blackout of faith, and prayers that seemed to get no answer? That the wind and the sea obey doesn't always mean that the storm is lifted. But there remains the power of a strange peace — the still point in the center, the eye of the hurricane — which Christ can give, and no one can explain.

Not long ago a young man came to see me and told me

quietly and unemotionally that he had only a year to live. Since he was aware that God had mysteriously given him a serenity and peace he wanted to express his gratitude by being baptized and confirmed in this church. He was without previous religious affiliation, by turn of mind a skeptic and utterly natural in his simple affirmations — neither mystical nor dogmatic. During the year which he still had to live, we talked more than once about his experience, and I suggested to him that he might put some of it on paper. He died before this could be more than a few scraps. But I have permission to read a little of what he said. The first sentences are: "These pages tell how almighty God in his infinite mercy made himself known to a dying man, and bore him up. But they are written in the hope that they may be read by some who disbelieve in God, or who, believing in God, disbelieve in the possibility of his acting in this way, and in the further hope that a few of those may be shaken in their disbelief."

He describes how shortly before he was given his medical ultimatum he found the fear of death lifted from him. The experience led him to thank God in prayer, but — in his own words — "I remember I did this without any sense of communication with God. In fact, I had no feeling of religiosity whatsoever during this period." Then, a week later, this happend to him: "Without any prior warning I underwent a religious experience. It followed upon the customary prayer...

It consisted of a conviction of the existence of God and of his goodness with respect to me and with respect to the balance of his creation. I saw nothing, heard nothing, felt nothing, and yet the experience was absolutely overwhelming." It was this that led him to a public confession of faith in Christ, and this that sustained him in the most amazing calm, common sense and even sparkling wit, right to the very end.

I tell this, not because we should all expect such vivid experiences of God's presence, but because here is a man, very much of this generation, who met the Christ beyond the storm. He was perfectly willing to discuss all the different psychological and physiological explanations of his experience, but, as he said, "this doesn't take me much further." His faith in God did.

Who can this be? For we meet him in the storm and find him when we get busy with what we call "Christian action." But we meet him also as he comes across the waves, walking on the water, saying: "Be of good cheer; it is I; be not afraid." The decision then is ours. What's the use of half measures? A little religion as a side bet? Jesus Christ, crucified in the storm, risen above the storm, holds out his hands to us. Can we not trust him *completely*?

II

Doing Your Thing:
Variety Without Anarchy

For just as in a single human body there are many limbs and organs, all with different functions, so all of us, united with Christ, form one body, serving individually as limbs and organs to one another.

ROMANS 12:4-5 (NEB)

One of the expressions that has recently filtered through from Hippieland to the rest of us is "doing your thing." It may not be elegant but it summarizes a philosophy of life with a brevity and clarity much nearer to the language of the Bible than to the gobbeldygook of modern sociology and religion. Moses, the psalmist, and the apostles would have understood what is meant by "doing your thing" while they might have been confused by an admonition to "structure their individuality abrasively in relation to environmental behavior patterns." In fact the word of St. Paul that we translate: "Be not conformed to this world" might very well read: "Do your thing."

To me there is something profoundly Christian in this philosophy of "doing your thing," and I believe

that at this point the older generation would do well
to stop criticizing for a moment and listen to the young.
They are crying out for a release of the true self, for
freedom from the conformities whereby many of us
are forced to do someone else's "thing." It seems to
them that our society stifles originality by setting
mediocre goals of material comfort and success to
which we sacrifice our souls. And if this seems to be
symbolized by the drab uniformity of the clothes we
wear, they find it natural to express themselves by
wearing what they like. I see no reason to deplore the
refreshing rash of color that enlivens our streets, or
the long-overdue reappearance of the male as the
"bird of plumage." But clothes and hair styles are
merely symptoms. The sign of hope is the revolt against
the obliteration of the individual in a society of mass-
production, mass media, and meaningless affluence.

Yet "doing your thing" is not merely an expression
of revolt. It suggests a new atmosphere of sincerity and
tolerance. Whatever reservations we may have about
some of the "things" young people do, we must welcome the respect they show to any sincere belief even
if it is quite unacceptable to them. I find that students
today may be just as resistant to the claims of the
Christian Church as they were a generation ago, but
there is far less hostility or scorn. The Church might
even learn from them to be less compromising in the
declaration of her basic beliefs. A minister is expected

to "do his thing" — which is to stand for "religion", for belief in God, in Christ, in prayer and worship. The Church is not admired when, in an attempt to win friends and influence people, we start doing someone else's "thing" — be it politics, psychiatry, or entertainment. We are expected to be concerned about all these, and to express the faith in new and unconventional ways, but fundamentally the Church's "thing" is, to use a theologically unfashionable word, "religion".

It would be good for us all if a respect for personal integrity, a willingness to let each one be himself, were to spread through all generations. We are all inclined to be chameleons, changing our color as we change environment — from home to business to church to club to the highway (where often a mild-mannered man becomes a fiend behind the wheel!). We're so afraid really to be ourselves that sometimes we wonder who we really are. One of the lessons of prisoner-of-war life, as I look back on it, was the gradual emergence of a tolerance that let each one "do his thing." At first we had the uniformity symbolized by our uniforms, but after a year or two we accepted without a comment any behavior that was not positively a menace to others. If one man I knew liked to sit half naked and cross-legged for hours on end on the top of his locker, nobody gave it a second thought. If another developed a passion for propelling a ping pong ball by his nose around the perimeter, or another unravelled socks, or collected beetles, or ate potato peelings mixed with German treacle — well, that was his "thing." More seriously, a great many found that the release from their normal civilian or military round freed them to discover the latent powers of their own souls.

Unfortunately there is a widespread belief that religion — and particularly membership in an organized church — is the enemy of such originality and freedom. And there are some grounds for this belief. We give the impression that church members are expected to conform to a pattern — to do the Church's "thing" and not their own. A church develops its image as conservative, liberal, radical, or middle-of-the-road, and people feel that, if they are to be members, they must be like-minded on all things. Worse than that, a curious aura of "churchiness" comes over normal men and women when they deal with the affairs of religion. They are often afraid to be their real selves, afraid that their own "thing" will not be acceptable. There are members who feel guilty because they are not naturally drawn to any of our church activities outside worship, and there are potential members who are held back because, although they consider themselves Christians, they don't want to be part of what seems to them to be this church's "thing". Again, there are others — and I have every sympathy with them — who fear that the gains of the ecumenical movement could be offset by the gradual elimination of those healthful, harmless differences that give life and color to our churches. In a huge super-church, bureaucratically organized, what room would there be for the individual or the congregation to "do their thing"?

If this is the impression we are making, if this is the trend in the modern church, then we are misrepresenting the message of the Bible and the Church of the New Testament. We have forgotten the ubiquitous evidence, in the story of creation and redemption, that God loves variety. The Bible itself is a compendium of astonishingly different writers ranging over the whole human scene in every conceivable literary mode. Because we bind it together in one volume, because there is an inspired unity in its central theme, because the glorious King James version imposes a kind of unity of style in the whole, we tend to miss the variety. In his interpretation of the standing dialogue between God and man each writer is left free to "do his own thing", and the Bible reflects everywhere God's delight in the infinite variety of his human family. It is a book of particulars, not generalities.

To begin at the beginning, have you ever thought of the doctrine of the Trinity as a symbol of variety in God himself? Our faith sees in the very heart of things a God who is not static, monotonous unity but the dynamic, creative love of Father, Son, and Holy Spirit. From this living God flows a continuous creation of the most astounding variety. Turn up a sod of

121

earth and we marvel at the multitude of squirming creatures we walk over every time we cross the Park. Think of the fantastic variety of fish in the oceans, of birds in the air, of beasts in the forest. Lie on your back in a summer night and the words of the Bible whisper to us that "one star differeth from another in glory." Then think of the family of man. I don't believe the generic term "humanity" ever occurs in the Bible. It may ask "What is man that thou art mindful of him," but only to assert that God indeed is mindful of us — of every single one in the long procession from the dawn of history. If the genealogies of the Bible, the long lists of "begats," seem to you a waste of space in our Holy Book, think of them as evidence that each individual matters to the Almighty who rejoices in the infinite variety of his human family. To believe in God's creation is to see a universe tingling with difference, where each throbbing atom, each circling planet, each creature from the ant to the hippopotamus, each individual human being, is "doing his thing."

If our belief in God's creation thus lights up a world of variety, what about our belief in redemption? I am talking about our Christian conviction that God rescues us from our sin and blindness and makes us a new creation in Christ Jesus. Sometimes we speak of this in such a way as to imply that to be a Christian, to accept this grace and become a living member of the Church, means that we lose our individuality. This is why some bold spirits are repelled by the thought of yielding their lives to Christ. They see Christian conversion as the abdication of their right to "do their thing", and the Christian Church as a community of the conforming.

But is it true that those who enter this Christian community, those who dedicate their lives as Christ's disciples are baptized into a standard pattern, and cease to be themselves? Right at the beginning, let's take a look at the men called to be disciples. There was no doubt about their devotion as they responded to the call. But was the result the elimination of their differences and the formation of a faceless, mindless group of religious nonentities? Were the blustering Peter, the bashful Andrew, the skeptical Thomas, the militants James and John, any less themselves *after* their call to discipleship? And can anyone read the Book of the Acts and suppose that members of the Christian Church settled comfortably into a mold? The whole New Testament is crowded with personalities, each one amazingly different, each one "doing his thing." So it has been with the saints of the Church. There are hardly two of them alike in temperament, interests, or way of life. The evidence is that genuine discipleship in any age makes a man or woman not less but more original, more a person, more utterly themselves.

123

This would not be so if becoming a Christian was a matter of accepting a book of rules, or giving the direction of one's life to some spiritual authority. What the Gospel offers is a spiritual grace that meets us just as we are. We are not asked to change ourselves into someone else. When the apostles wrote of being "justified by faith," they meant that God accepted them as they were without demanding any preliminary religious reformation of character. Christ surprised the religious leaders of his day precisely by his acceptance of a huge variety of people — just as they were. And to this day he does not look for some particular kind of people to be members of his Church. God creates us in abundant variety; and he redeems us with all our originality and difference.

So, says St. Paul, don't think of the Church as an organization of the temperamentally religious, but as the Body of Christ on earth. "For just as in a single human body there are many limbs and organs, all with different functions, so all of us, united with Christ, form one body, serving individually as limbs and organs to one another." What can be more different in shape and size and function than an ear, an eye, a nose, a leg? Each one, thank God, does its own thing — otherwise we should soon be in the doctor's hands. Have we really heard this about our membership in the Church? This is where the word "member" comes from: it should suggest variety rather than sameness.

124

Christ wants *you* in his Church — not some imitation you, striving to do someone else's thing.

So it's variety, variety, variety, from creation through redemption to the end of the story. For I would remind you that in Christian symbolism it is heaven not hell that is the condition of infinite variety. "In my Father's house are many mansions." And it is hell not heaven that is the place of fearful monotony — for there is no deadlier monotony than sin. (There is ultimately only one way of breaking a "Thou shalt not;" but there are a million ways of fulfilling the positive commandment to love God and our neighbor.)

Does all this mean, then, that "doing your thing" is an absolute, that variety is not only the spice of life but its one supreme rule? How about the clash that comes when my variety interferes with yours, when by doing my thing I hinder you from doing yours? Let me swing back for a moment and see how variety is truly fostered and enjoyed.

What, we must ask, is the basis of the magnificent variety of creation, the profusion of Nature's gifts? Is it chaos or cosmos? There is little doubt about the answer. The Genesis poet saw it very clearly. *Before* creation he sees chaos. "The earth was without form and void." Then came cosmos, order and within that cosmos the huge variety developed. Modern science reveals to us not only the bewildering multiplicity of life, but the astonishing order that permeates creation.

125

It is that order — what we have been used to call the "laws of nature" — that makes possible the infinite variety. Without it everything would collapse.

What is true of Nature is equally true of human nature. The Bible speaks of other laws, the cosmos of human behavior, and every human society has evolved some kind of rules within which the individual is set free to "do his thing." The plain truth is that anarchy, (which is the abolition of all rules) far from expanding freedom, destroys it. Without the coherence of an ordered society there is no possibility of "doing one's thing." This is the paradox we proclaim when we speak of the "service which is perfect freedom." It is not so hard to understand. Would a trombone player in an orchestra be more free to "do his thing" if there were no conductor to impose order, no score to be followed? Would a great tennis player be more free to "do his thing" if we abolished the rules of the game?

"All of us, *united with Christ*, form one body." I have spoken of the Church as the community of variety where we should be more, not less, free to be ourselves, and "do our thing." But the metaphor of the body where each member has a quite different function, depends on the unity and order without which there can be no living organism. The head, the center, the source of order in a Christian community is Christ. Without allegiance to him we cannot be truly free. St. Augustine's summary of Christian ethics

— "Love God and do what you will" — is often quoted today as if it meant that all rules are abolished and we can "do our thing" in blissful disregard of the commandments. Surely the time has come for the Church to declare more unambiguously that loving God comes first; that without an acceptance of the discipline of discipleship we are not ready to "do our thing".

I began by saying that we should listen to the young when they urge us to cease conforming to meaningless patterns and to "do our thing." I would end by saying that the time has come for all, young and old, to think again about the indispensable basis of our freedom — which is order and discipline. Without them we shall not have more freedom but the anarchy that makes all true variety impossible. To express our dissent from human authority is the heritage of free men and women in a democratic society. To "do our thing" in flagrant violation of the laws of such a society is to point the way to a state of anarchy in which freedom dies.

The function of the Church at such a time must be to proclaim and to demonstrate the presence of a God who loves variety and is the source of order, and of a Christ who accepts us as we are, and brings us into a community where we each "do our thing" guided by his Spirit in the unity of his Body.

12

Is God Unfair?

Why be jealous because I am kind?
                    ST. MATTHEW 20:15 (NEB)

"Unfair" is one of the basic words in the English language. It expresses something more than an abstract sense of justice. The ideas of "fair play," "fair dealing," "fair wages," "fair practice," arouse our very deepest emotions, and anything that violates our sense of what is fair can touch off the most passionate protest. "Unfair" is such an expressive word that other languages — like German — have simply adopted it without translation.

Behind many of the disputes disrupting society lies the question of what is fair. What settlement of the school controversy will be fair both to the teachers and to those who are committed to the experiment of local community control? What is fair pay for a policeman, a fireman, a garbage collector? Are we being fair to the children, to the old people? What is fair taxation? What is the fairest way to grant relief or to allocate hospital beds? No wonder the word "unfair" turns up again and again in speeches, pamphlets and picket signs.

We can't, as Christian citizens, wash our hands and say, "Thank God I'm not in charge." If the great

128

Bible words "justice" and "communion" mean anything to us we must be concerned with fair solutions to every problem that threatens the health of the community. So we try to learn the facts, to avoid hasty judgments and to encourage the mediators and reconcilers. The highest compliment that can be paid to anyone who tries to arbitrate any dispute is that he is fair. Even in the most uninhibited period of infighting in the presidential election, the average citizen tries to keep his judgment intact as to what is fair tactics and what is not.

But we are not always calm judges in other men's disputes. From early childhood we find ourselves responding violently to what strikes us as unfair — especially when our own rights are concerned. Has there ever been a family where parents have not heard the cry: "It's unfair!"? It's one of the first words we learn. And you will have noticed how quickly we descend from the platform of calm arbitration when our own interests come into the picture. We can be cool and reasonable judges of a neighbor's controversy with his children or of disputes like that between India and Pakistan or even Israel and the Arabs or Nigeria and Biafra, but the moment we sense an injustice to ourselves or our particular group or nation we are soon aroused to passion.

The Bible knows all about this ideal and this passion. The recurring words in Old and New Testament — justice and righteousness — have both to do with what we call fair play. We are shown without any pious falsification a world where a great deal that happens seems manifestly unfair and yet the God who is responsible is held to be absolutely just, the one who is, as the psalmist says, "the righteous Lord," who "loveth righteousness" or, as we would say, a God who is absolutely fair and expects us to be the same. The word that Abraham heard when he pleaded for the city of Sodom rings through the Bible as the ultimate conviction of the man of faith, no matter how sorely tried: "Shall not the Judge of all the earth do right?".

Christ knew very well that there is no simple way of demonstrating the fairness of God. And he was aware of the extreme difficulty of deciding what is fair play among men. So we don't find any quick answers to our questions either about the fairness of life as we know it, or about the disputes that arise between men. When he was asked about the victims of two horrible incidents in his time — the massacre of a group of Jews by Pilate's soldiers and the collapse of the tower of Siloam — his answer was both blunt and cryptic: "Do you imagine that they were more guilty than all the other people living in Jerusalem? I tell you they were not; but unless you repent, you will all of you come to the same end." And when he was asked to intervene in a fraternal dispute over an inheritance he simply said: "My good man, who set me over you to judge or arbitrate?". Then he said to the people: "Beware! Be on your guard against greed of every kind."

So we should not be surprised that he told a tantalizing story about a labor dispute to set us thinking about the fairness or unfairness of God.

The parable of the laborers in the vineyard offers a classic example of our difficulty in deciding what is fair. Frankly, whose side are you on? The argument of the men who had worked all day is extremely powerful. They had labored from sunrise to sunset, "sweating," as they put it, "the whole day long in the blazing sun." And then they watched the men who had put in a bare hour's work receiving exactly the same pay. If ever there was a case for a differential, this was it! In our day such a situation could well be the signal for a wild-cat strike. Unfair! But what is the master's answer? It is a straightforward appeal to legality and justice. There was a contract. They had agreed to work all day for one denarius. They got their denarius. The others had no contract, and what they received was no one's business but the master's. Is there anything unfair about getting what you agreed to accept? We have to remember that in those days there were no unions or acts of Congress regulating labor relations. So the clincher came with the words: "Surely I am free to do what I like with my own money? Why be jealous because I am kind?".

This is what is called a "parable of the Kingdom." That means that Christ is answering a question about the nature of the Kingdom of God. And the particular question that sparked this parable had to do with God's acceptance of the class known as "publicans and sinners" on equal, or even preferential terms with the devout. The big scandal of Christ's ministry was his welcome extended to the disreputable, the irreligious and the socially unacceptable the moment they showed a desire for the new life he was offering. The religious were horrified. It was so unfair. "Here we have been slaving away at prayers and sacrifices," they said, "for years and years and now we are told that these Johnny-come-latelies get into the Kingdom along with, or even ahead of us." The devout in every age are liable to this resentment against the acceptance of newcomers who have discovered Christ in their own way and responded to his Gospel. For there lingers somewhere in the back of the mind of many good churchmen the thought that God must reward them for their devotion. Wasn't this the point Jesus made also in the story of the Prodigal Son? The elder brother complained bitterly that his father was unfair. "Lo, these many years do I serve thee, neither transgressed I at any time thy commandment: and yet thou never gavest me a kid that I might make merry with my friends: but as soon as this thy son has come, which hath devoured thy living with harlots, thou hast killed for him the fatted calf." The answer could have come in the exact words of our text: "Why be jealous because I am kind?".

When we think further about the apparent unfairness of God's dealings with men, the parable begins to throw light into some very dark corners of our experience. What are we to make of the contrast between the successful scoundrel and the decent man who is ruined through no fault of his own? Why is it that so often the very finest men and women we know become the victims of accidents or disease? Why are nations seeking freedom crushed by sheer brute force? Why does God allow blow after blow to fall on those who are among the most truly Christian that we know? The psalmists asked these questions about the fairness of God. So did Job. So did the great dramatists and novelists of every age. Which one of us has not at some time or other cried out against the apparent unfairness of God? What's the answer?

Let me tell you briefly two things this parable says to me.

(1). No matter how we may genuinely revolt against the unfairness of life (and the Bible encourages us to express our feelings), we can trust in the absolute justice of God. He will stand by his word. He will do what is right. "I will pay you a fair wage." We must remember that God sees the whole story from beginning to end. We are like those who come in for the second act of a play and leave before the end. We don't hear the whole story. And the story of human life and destiny is, according to the Bible, played out on a larger stage than that of this world. It is in the light of eternity that God's justice and fairness will be seen. Let me say frankly

133

that if I did not believe in an afterlife, I would find it hard, if not impossible, to believe in the fairness of God. I don't mean this as a kind of easy way out — "Things are so messed up here they're bound to be sorted out somewhere else." I only know that at moments of great tragedy when even a pastor can find no words to say, I have been conscious of that eternal goodness and a justice beyond our sight. Do you know T. S. Eliot's words at the end of "Little Gidding"?

> "A condition of complete simplicity
> (costing not less than everything)
> And all shall be well and
> All manner of thing shall be well
> When the tongues of flame are in-folded
> Into the crowned knot of fire
> And the fire and the rose are one."

(2). But — and here we touch the heart of the Gospel — God is more than fair. The whole teaching of Jesus converges on this truth. He is not just the God who gives us our deserts: He is the God who pours a love on us that we cannot possibly deserve. That's why Jesus shocked so many with his actions and his stories; for he dismissed the idea that men can make a claim on God by reason of their goodness. For him God is not a celestial bookkeeper allotting points to each of us for our prayers and our good deeds, and subtracting for every lapse from the moral code. He just tells us that we are all, in our own way, sinners; and that the relative guilt is not our business but God's. And then he tells us that God is waiting to receive everyone on the same basis — just a confession of need and an acceptance of grace. That's what we do here. We don't come to the Lord's table graded according to some scale of goodness. We all come as sinners, and we all receive the same bread and wine, the symbols of his grace.

So this is the place where we realize the amazing kindness of God. It is not the place where we judge one another and complain that others have treated us badly and have no right to the grace of God. He is more than fair to everyone of us as he pours into us the grace of the Lord Jesus Christ and the communion of the Spirit. Here is where bitterness and jealousy can be burned out of our hearts, for the voice is near: "Why be jealous because I am kind?".

There may be all kinds of questions and protests in our minds or hearts about the unfairness of life. But there is one thought that must quell them in the Christian believer. What do you think has been the most agonizingly unfair act in the whole story of mankind? Was it not the torture and death of Jesus of Nazareth? Nothing we know can match the injustice and unfairness of that crucifixion of a young and innocent life. This is God's final answer to our charge. He takes the unfairness on himself. His Son suffers, "the just for the unjust" to bring us to the Father. Christ has borne our sins. Is that fair? It was more than fair. It was the devastating love of a God who exposes himself to the jealousies and hates of men and in Christ now offers us a pardon and a peace that we have not deserved. The God we meet in holy communion is not only fair, he is infinitely kind.

13
Labor, Leisure and Worship

Six days shalt thou labour, and do all thy work: But the seventh day is the sabbath of the Lord thy God.

EXODUS 20:9, 10

When preachers or politicians tell us today that what this country needs is to get back to a respect for the Ten Commandments, many wag their heads in solemn agreement. Not so many turn up the record to see just exactly what the Commandments require. When they do I should be surprised if they don't find some trouble with the fourth: "Six days shalt thou labour, and do all thy work: But the seventh day is the sabbath of the Lord thy God."

As it stands this commandment plainly refers to the Jewish Sabbath — Saturday in our week. It demands that this day be set apart from the six days of a working week. No work on the seventh day — that is the law. If then, we profess to respect the Ten Commandments and believe that they are a solid moral foundation for today, as well as the past, what are we to do about this commandment? If a modern teenager, hearing you commend the Ten Commandments, were to say: "O.K., just how do I begin keeping Saturday holy?", what would be your reply?

There are roughly three ways in which Christians can deal with this question. (For our Jewish friends the matter is naturally less complicated.)

(1). We can interpret the commandment quite literally — in which case we have to say that, unlike all the other commandments, this one is not of universal application. It belongs, with all the other ritual requirements in the Old Testament, to the Judaism that has not been held binding on the Christian Church. Whereas the other commandments — about worship, idolatry, blasphemy, reverence for parents, murder, adultery, theft, false witness and covetousness — express what you might almost call the moral consensus of mankind, soaring far beyond both Judaism and Christianity, this one about the sabbath seems quite definitely dated and parochial. So some would say that it has no more application to the non-Jew than circumcision or the kosher diet, and should, therefore, be omitted from the commandments of universal application. The only Christians who accept the commandment literally, and seek to obey it, are the Seventh Day Adventists, who, as their name implies, observe Saturday and not Sunday as their holy day. But the Adventists' argument, difficult though it is to refute on any literalist reading of the Bible, has failed to convince the vast majority of Christians throughout the ages.

(2). The traditional way of interpreting the fourth commandment in the Christian Church — and partic-

ularly in our Reformed tradition — has been to identify
the Jewish sabbath with our Sunday, the Lord's day.
Some of us can remember when Presbyterians talked of
"Sabbath Worship", "the Sabbath School" and "Sabbath observance". And some can remember a very strict
interpretion of the fourth commandment along these
lines. I can recall being rebuked by a puritanical Irish
grandmother for whittling a stick one Sunday afternoon.
"What are you doing?" she asked. "Making a ship," I
replied. "They must be hard up for ships," she
snapped, "if they have to make them on the sabbath
day." I suppose the incident may have sparked my first
theological thinking, for now after fifty years I have to
report that I find no justification whatever for supposing
that what is said here about the sabbath can be simply
transferred to the Christian Sunday.

Sunday is, of course, a pagan name. The first Chist-
ians referred to the Lord's Day, the day of Christ's
resurrection, the first day of the week. It was a day of
worship from the earliest years of the Church. They
said nothing about it being a rest day, a sabbath. It
was a day for coming together to praise God and com-
mune with Christ. The fourth commandment, you
will notice, says nothing about worship. If you divide
the commandments into those that refer to our duty
to God and those that refer to our duty to our fellow
men, it clearly belongs with the latter. "Thou shalt not
do any work, thou, nor thy son, nor thy daughter, nor

139

thy manservant, nor thy maidservant, nor thy cattle,
nor thy stranger that is within thy gates." (You will
notice that the missing person is mother — the Bible
knows how much housework she may have to do!) This
is a humanitarian commandment — among other things
a charter of emancipation for the working man. The
sabbath is primarily the day of rest. Sunday is the day
of worship. The two can be related, but simply cannot
be identified. For centuries the Christian Sunday was,
of necessity, both the rest day and the worship day. I
suggest that with the advent of the five day week most
Church people today are in a position to observe both
the sabbath and the Sunday. They have their day for
rest and recreation — and they have their day for
worship and Christian service.

(3). Now we can see perhaps the real force of this
commandment, and why it is something much more
than a Jewish ritual requirement. It is set among the
great moral precepts to which every civilization has
responded to remind us of the divine rhythm of work
and rest, labor and leisure and to illuminate their meaning. It speaks of the universal obligation to work for
our living and of the absolute necessity of a weekly
pause for leisure and recreation. In almost every part
of the world some such provision is made, and it is interesting to note that every experiment in the West to
alter the rhythm of one day in seven has broken down.
The whole weight of this commandment was on the

alleviation of human toil, the provision of time off for those who were subject to hard-driving masters. So far from being a burdensome piece of religious legislation, it was a charter of emancipation centuries ahead of its time. The kind of rights that early trade unionists had to fight for were already proclaimed in the fourth commandment. A major point of dispute between Christ and the religious establishment was precisely this — that he loved the sabbath as God's great gift to man while they, like many of our own ancestors, had made it an additional burden on his back. That's the insight of his liberating words: "The sabbath was made for man, and not man for the sabbath."

"Six days shalt thou labour, and do all thy work." The Bible has a great deal to say about work, some of it quite surprising. In the first place, the ancient world found it odd that religion and work should be related at all. For the Greek the ideal was to be able to live a life of culture and philosophizing, leaving the necessary work to be done by slaves and servants. For them, on the whole, work was ignoble and degrading. And this Greek notion possessed aristocratic societies in the West straight down to our own times. The Bible puts its demand for work right in among its central commandments for worship and social ethics. It goes even farther, for it grounds the dignity of work in the image of a working God. "For in six days the Lord made heaven and earth, the sea, and all that in them is." This

141

imaginative use of the creation myth is enormously powerful. (Only a literalist gets hung up here on the "six days", as only a literalist would insist that "six days shalt thou labour" is an argument against the five-day week!) Our God is a worker. He creates. His energy is everywhere. And man, made in his image, is a creator too — whether of harvests and homes, implements and vehicles, goods and services or books and paintings. So the Christian can understand when he learns that the Son of God lived on earth as a carpenter, and not as a gentleman of leisure.

Yet the moment we begin to talk today about the dignity of labor or the joy of creativity, in all honesty we have to remember the millions whose work is dull and monotonous or so routine as to be robbed of all sense of creation. It's easy to talk romantic nonsense from the pulpit and forget that one is not always speaking to men and women who can find joy and purpose in their daily labor. In my first parish I was talking to farm workers and country people who had a real sense of meaning in their work, but at the same time a friend of mine went to a parish where one third of his congregation were employed checking coupons for the football-pool gambling industry. I remember him remarking on the difficulty in talking about vocation and God-given meaning in daily labor! We have to confess that a great deal of modern work, whatever its value to the community, is routine, and that even the most interesting and the most creative occupations have their quota of drudgery and days of sheer weariness and toil.

This is also very frankly recognized in the Bible. The Genesis stories don't just speak of man's joy in creative labor as he is given dominion over the earth. With the story of the Fall comes the other side of the coin. "Cursed is the ground for thy sake; in sorrow shalt thou eat of it all the days of thy life; thorns and thistles shall it bring forth to thee... in the sweat of thy face shalt thou eat bread." I take this to mean that we have no right to expect that labor will always be lit with joy and fascination. We have to accept the sweat. Thus, in a similar realistic vein, Paul tells the Thessalonian Christians, some of whom had given up their daily jobs in expectation of the Lord's early return, that he himself had "toiled and drudged" to earn his living, and that "the man who will not work shall not eat". The Christian then is to hold all honest labor in high honor, but at the same time accept the element of sheer toil and drudgery. Simultaneously he experiences the redemptive grace whereby all work — even the most menial — can be offered to God as acceptable worship. *Laborare est orare.* To work is to pray.

Then what about leisure? "The seventh day is the sabbath of the Lord thy God." This too, you will note, is rooted in the life of God himself. "The Lord rested." However we understand that, the Bible indicates everywhere that God is not only the Worker: there is in

him that which corresponds to relaxation and rest. We
in the West have lived with the picture of a very busy
God. That's one of the reasons why the West has been
the dynamic, progressive section of humanity — the
Judaeo-Christian tradition has impelled it. But we
might learn something from the East where there is a
deeper sense of God's repose. The One who says: "Be
still, and know that I am God." is inviting us to the
cosmic quiet, the divine détente which is as real as the
holy energy that moves the world.

Once we see the connection between leisure and
God, we shall not be tempted to associate our times of va-
cation, or our weekly rest and recreation, with what you
might call a "holiday from God". He is as concerned
with our leisure as with our labor. *Ludere est orare.* In a
real sense, to play is to pray. So the man who tells me:
"I can worship God as well on the golf course as in
church" is entirely right. The pertinent comment is, of
course, do you? Do we really have a sense of God's
presence in our recreations? Have we forgotten that a
holiday is literally a holy day?

I remarked that, contrary to what many people
think, there is nothing said about worship in the fourth
commandment. It speaks of labor and leisure — the
necessity of work and the necessity of a day without
work. The reason for this is that the Bible doesn't
shunt religion off into a special section labeled "for
sabbath day only." The entire table of commandments

is headed: "I am the Lord thy God." The summary of
the law begins: "Thou shalt worship the Lord thy God."
The whole of life, work and play, is to be lived under
God, and offered to him in worship. But, just as we
should love and honor our parents at all times yet feel
the need for special times of remembrance, so we are
unlikely to live our whole life under God unless we
set apart such times to offer to him alone. Thus within
the space granted us when we do not have to work, we
make room for the public worship of God. And from
that bright point of concentrated worship a holy light
will fall on all the activities both of our work and our
leisure.

I suggested that it is easier for us to keep both a
sabbath of rest and recreation and a Sunday of worship
and Christian service than it was for our forefathers.
But the pace of change in society now indicates that the
problem for the future will not be to carve out time
from work for recreation and for worship, but how to
cope with life when machines take over and leisure
vastly increases. This may seem academic to many of
us in our busy round today, but the indications are
that the four-day, the three-day, perhaps the one-day
working week may not be far away for millions. Can
we continue to find guidance in commandments com-
posed for a totally different state of affairs? "Six days
shalt thou labour, and do all thy work: But the seventh
day is the sabbath of the Lord thy God." What validity

will that have twenty years from now?

There's a phrase in a hymn we sing about "the endless sabbaths the blessed ones see." As a small boy in my grandmother's house I was not much attracted by the prospect of "endless sabbaths." But once we've disentangled ourselves from the image of the "sabbath" as a day of dullness and restrictions and begun to see it as God's great gift to man, perhaps we may find that this old word offers a clue to what many are beginning to call "the problem of leisure." For "sabbath" means leisure that is positive, filled with meaning and delight.

When we are told in the same breath that the immediate future holds the prospect of an enormous increase of non-working hours *and* a withering away of religion, then we can only say: "God help the human race." For it is precisely the gifts that a living faith can bring which will make tolerable the huge extension of leisure. I saw that in prison camps during World War II. Suddenly a group of normally active, hard-working men had great stretches of time to dispose of. Those who found it most tolerable were those whose horizons were not limited to this secular world. In a world without God free time can be hell. You can't spend five years playing bridge — though I know some who tried. For the believer such free time can, on occasion, be a foretaste of heaven. For it means the development of creative gifts, and exploration of prayer and worship and the discovery of the hidden worlds of the spirit.

146

We need to learn now the art of the sabbath as the time for true re-creation of body, soul and spirit. The busy worker — whatever his occupation — needs to learn that art now if retirement is not to be a misery. The world of modern industry needs to learn that art now, if automation is not to produce in the near future a national neurosis. And every one of us needs to learn that art if eternal life is to be for us a heaven of endless adventure rather than a hell of boredom.

"The seventh day is the sabbath of the Lord thy God." When that becomes "fourth, fifth, sixth and seventh", it will be all the more, not less, necessary for us to know what that sabbath really means. For it contains the secret of leisure — the development from within, the expansion of the soul, the discovery of divine resources, the "exploration unto God."

14

Pro-Existence

Bear ye one another's burdens, and so fulfil the law of Christ. GALATIANS 6:2

After an infant has been baptized in our service here, the minister says: "This child is now received into the holy catholic Church." Why do we say that? Because Baptism is a sacrament of the Church Universal. The holy catholic Church is the world-wide communion of Christians, holding the apostolic faith. It is the company of those who, with their children, confess Jesus Christ as Lord and Savior. In our service of Baptism we don't make infants into little Presbyterians or little Protestants. We declare them to be members of that inclusive family of which Christ is Head. Baptism is thus a great uniting sacrament in which the dividing labels fall away — perhaps the one point today at which the word "catholic" shines out in its purest and deepest meaning.

In popular speech, however, "catholic" means "Roman Catholic," and to save my time and your patience I am going to use it in that sense today. For I am going to speak about the relationship of Protestant and Catholic in today's world and what I believe to be the call of God as we face together the greatest challenge to the Christian faith and way of life since the fourth century of the Christian era.

My thesis is simply this: That in the social, moral and religious upheaval through which we are living, the common beliefs, the common values, the common burdens and the common experience of God's grace are infinitely more important than the matters that divide us, and that to an extent we may not yet have realized, Protestants and Catholics need each other in this hour of crisis. The Word of God to us is, therefore: "Bear ye one another's burdens, and so fulfil the law of Christ."'

Let me make it clear that I am *not* talking about some process by which Protestants and Catholics can reverse the fateful decisions of the sixteenth century and move towards an institutional merger. How ever deeply we cherish the ideal of one visible and united Body of Christ on earth — a Church with no adjective attached — we must be realistic. It is hard enough to persuade Protestant denominations of similar tradition to re-unite. Humanly speaking, it would seem almost impossible to achieve a united Church in which all Catholics and Protestants would find themselves at home without compromising some of their deepest convictions. Let ecumenical conversations continue in spite of the huge theological hurdles and the counter-tide that is now bucking the whole movement. The conviction is growing in me that events are going to overtake the ecumenical movement as we know it now. The next twenty years may see such catastrophic shifts and

149

re-alignment of religious forces in the world that our present controversies may seem totally irrelevant. That's why I am bypassing the question of ultimate reunion to speak of the immediate summons to all Christian people to seek from God a common strength to confront a world that is rapidly discarding the most basic beliefs we have long held in common.

So far we have passed through two stages of Protestant-Catholic relations. From the explosion of the Reformation for about two centuries, there was the period of polemics. Each side anathematized the other, and choice expressions such as "arch-heretic," "apostate," "Devil's disciple," "ministers of Satan," "scarlet woman" and "whore of Babylon" were freely used. (You will find echoes of this period in the confessions we retain among the subordinate standards of the Church.) The theological battle erupted, to the eternal shame of Christendom, in armed conflict, and only the compromise of allowing each ruler to decide the religion of his state finally ended the Thirty Years' War.

The next period, lasting — I would estimate — till the recent Vatican Council has been the period of co-existence. The polemics died down although kept alive by fanatics on either side. You might say that, by and large, Protestant and Catholic churches ignored each other while agreeing to live in peace. The situation was not unlike that which prevailed between Christians and

Moslems after the fury of the crusades and the Moslem invasion of Europe. Not many were looking for a fight, and there was a tacit agreement to live and let live. But the assumption was that Protestantism and Catholicism were two entirely different religions. (I once counselled with a young girl from the north of Ireland, who was proposing to marry a Moslem. After going into all the problems of such a mixed marriage, I asked what her father thought about it. "Well," she said, "he was a bit worried, but in the end he said: 'Sure, it might have been worse; he might have been a Catholic'!") When I came to New York twelve years ago, I was struck by the fact that, while I heard little anti-Catholic talk, there seemed no contact whatever between the two communions in the city. We coexisted — without even fully accepting each other as fellow Christians.

In recent years it has come home to me with increasing force, that mere coexistence is an intolerable policy for Christian people. The word belongs to the politics of the cold war, not to communities of men and women pledged to a common Lord, and the reconciling Gospel He has committed to us all. Peter and Paul, and the other apostles had their differences — sometimes quite strident but can you imagine what would have happened if they and their followers had merely agreed to co-exist? Could coldly coexisting Christians have carried the Gospel across the Roman world or withstood the savage persecution of these early days? Do you think

151

coexistence is enough for Catholics and Protestants today living in the Communist lands of eastern Europe? And does anyone imagine that we are living here in a time of such religious and moral stability that the two great representatives of the Christian tradition can continue to go their own ways in silent competition for the souls of men?

The word for today is not coexistence but *pro*-existence. By pro-existence I mean literally existing *for* each other — in the apostle's words "bearing one another's burdens." This is the policy demanded not only by the spiritual crisis in the modern world, but by the Lord, himself: "Bear ye one another's burdens, and so fulfil the law of Christ." What is this law of Christ? Nothing could be plainer: "This is my commandment, That ye love one another, as I have loved you" (St. John 15:12). Without in any way repudiating the witness of our Protestant ancestors and the true glories of the Reformation, we are now summoned to slam the door on all recrimination and suspicion, all jealousy and bitterness, all prejudice and fear and to live *for* and not *against* each other through these years of turmoil, and spiritual revolution.

Words like "crisis," and "turmoil" are perhaps overworked today, but it is doubtful if any of us has yet grasped the full extent of the revolution they represent. It is easy to read backwards and recognize periods like that of the fall of the Roman Empire, the Reformation,

152

the French Revolution, as mighty turning points in our history. It is not so easy to recognize a revolution when you are in it. Yet the signs are around us to indicate that future historians (if there are any) will label this period as the prelude to the greatest revolution of all. What exactly is happening and whether the end result will be catastrophe and dissolution or a new stage in a God-guided evolution of humanity, no one can say. One thing seems to be clearer every day: We are watching the complete breakdown of the cluster of values — our inheritance from Judaism, Christianity and Hellenism — that sustained what we call the civilization of the West. The moral and spiritual axioms on which our fathers depended, whether or not they obeyed them, are vanishing. Everything is questioned; everything is in flux. There is not a single assumption of the past that is now sheltered from the winds of change. There is no accepted authority, no unspoken consensus about right and wrong. The established generation is unsure of itself, fumbling and guilt-ridden. The revolutionary generation knows what it wants to overthrow but not what it wants to construct. Yet through the confusion we sense a yearning for a new world that will not be simply the product of our technology but something nearer to what the creed calls "the communion of saints."

It is in this pregnant situation that Protestants and Catholics need each other as never before. Faced with a world where our common assumptions are rejected, where a new kind of humanity is struggling to be born, where anarchy or totalitarianism are just round the corner for any nation, no matter how apparently secure, can we ignore each other any longer? Can we indulge in petty infighting and rivalry? Can we find nothing better to do than to discuss just how infallible an infallible Pope can be or what titles to give the Mother of our Lord? I am not asking for an abandonment of theological discussion or an ignoring of the clash of conscience and conviction that·divides sincere Christians. But I am asking for *pro*-existence, a new spirit of understanding, sympathy and the deepest possible spiritual communion and loyalty to the one Lord and Head of the Church.

"Bear ye one another's burdens, and so fulfil the law of Christ." What are the burdens of the Protestant and Catholic today? Let me mention one that is among the heaviest. It is a burden that is common to both communions though it takes a different shape. I am thinking of the crisis of belief and confidence within the Church itself.

It is folly to imagine that either Protestants or Catholics stand like solid rocks of faith in the spiritual storm. The winds of change and the waves of skepticism are sweeping through every religious institution. It is hard for us who were raised to think of the Roman Catholic Church as a vast monolith of unshakable religious authority to believe our ears and eyes when we realize what is happening today. Those who, while unable to accept the demands of that church, looked on it as a kind of bastion of our civilization, are appalled by the sudden tremor in the foundations — the spirit of revolt that has appeared even in the inner citadel of the clergy. One symptom is the accelerating exodus of priests into the secular world and the radical questions that are being raised in the seminaries.

This is not a situation that we can regard with complacent satisfaction — as if what is at stake is the authority of Rome. This upheaval and agony of faith is our burden too. The future of the whole Christian Church is at stake. Don't imagine for a moment that the priests who walk out of the Catholic Church come running happily to the Protestants. They do not. They are, for the most part, either accepting a totally secular world where faith is an illusion, or else they are seeking a religion that is free from any system or institution, Catholic or Protestant. This burden of our Catholic brethren is one we must accept as our burden as we pray with them for God's guidance in the burning question concerning the limits of authority and of freedom. Their agony is our agony in the common task of renewing the Church today. (It makes me happy, for instance, to hear that a sermon from this pulpit found its way into a Catholic seminary and helped to prevent young men abandoning their vocation.)

This particular burden in the Catholic Church is, of course, related to the authoritarian tradition and the close-knit theological system that goes with it. Thus doubt on a minor point of faith can sometimes lead to a collapse of the entire fabric. It is this that we must try sympathetically to understand and so refrain from nasty judgments on the assumption that the rebels are always right.

The Protestant burden in the crisis of faith is different from the Catholic but equally heavy. Our problem is not an excess of authority and discipline but the reverse. We face the spiritual turmoil with divided ranks, conflicting voices and a desperate lack of spiritual power. We have to confess that we have abused our freedom through rank sectarianism, individualism — each man his own church — and a fearful neglect of the discipline in discipleship. Too many Protestants who scorn the "compulsion of the Mass" expresses their freedom by neglecting the public worship of their God. Too many Protestants who object to prayers to the saints have ceased to pray to anyone at all. Too many Protestants who dislike the politics of Rome are trying to make their own churches little more than social and political pressure groups. And too many Protestants who hate the smell of incense are content with the stale odors of the secular world. We have tremendous need for discipline, devotion and a revival of pure faith in

Christ as we go about his task of reconciliation in the world around us.

For surely Father Gregory Baum is right when he says that God's call to fellowship and harmony is a priority for the Church in our divided world. Hence, the immediate obligation on us all is to close ranks in a reconciling spirit within the Chistian Church. How can we minister the Gospel of reconciliation in this hate-filled society if we have not learned first "to bear one another's burdens, and so fulfil the law of Christ"? Now is the time to pro-exist — to minimize our differences and maximize our common faith.

We may not have much time. The currents of secularism, non-Christian humanism and a quasi-religious nationalism are running high and fast. Protestants and Catholics need each other in the search for the true balance between authority and freedom, between tradition and innovation, between piety and action. We must learn to share our problems as we share a conviction about where the answer is to be found. In the future let our only competition be in loyalty to the Lord who is the final authority in his Church. It is that loyalty we seek to revive in our church. It is that loyalty we rejoice to see in our Catholic neighbors. Do you see what it means that in a distressed and confused generation there exists a body of men and women who despite all differences of belief and practice can say together: "I believe in God the Father almighty, and in Jesus Christ

157

his only Son our Lord," and "I believe in the Holy
Ghost, the Lord and Giver of life."?

15

The Making
of a Christian

*Agrippa said to Paul, "You think it will not take much
to win me over and make a Christian of me."*

ACTS 26:28 (NEB)

Let me introduce the speaker: King Herod Agrippa II,
last in line of a series of artful and unscrupulous politicians who made their fortunes as dishonest brokers
between the Jews and the early Roman emperors. This
man, Agrippa, was a kind of quisling prince who had
recently added to his dominions a portion of Galilee
by ingratiating himself with the Emperor Nero. Bernice,
the queen at his side, was his sister with whom he had
incestuous relations. She was later the mistress of
Titus, the general who destroyed Jerusalem. The family
life of the Herods, of whom five are mentioned in the
New Testament, would provide a lifetime of material
for a modern scandal sheet, and this Agrippa was
perhaps the toughest specimen since Herod the Great.

This, then, was the man who looked St. Paul in the
face and said with a smooth irony: "You think it will
not take much to win *me* over and make a Christian of
me." Paul's answer rings with the assurance and

159

audacity of the early Church. Who knows how much or how little it would take to make this regal ruffian a Christian — that's God's business. His own fervent desire was the same for him as for the meanest of his slaves. "I wish to God that not only you, but all those also who are listening to me today, might become what I am — apart from these chains."

"With that," we read, "the king rose," and while Paul was still rattling his chains the elegant visitors withdrew. The hearing was over. It had not been an official investigation but an occasion dreamed up by Festus the Roman the night before. King Agrippa and Queen Bernice were paying a state visit and the two men had been talking politics after dinner. The governor had told the king about the interesting prisoner he had on his hands and his difficulty in knowing how to deal with the case. So Agrippa had said: "I'd rather like to hear the man myself." That's how Paul found himself transferred from his cell to the gorgeous stateroom with its glittering assembly of "high-ranking officers and prominent citizens," surrounded by the pomp and ceremony of both Romans and Herodians. As he looked around him this extraordinary man evidently didn't see the majestic robes, the gleaming jewels, the array of top, top brass; nor did he see what we would call the Establishment, the "power-structure" in its Sunday clothes. He saw human beings. And he saw a congregation. That was just what he wanted. So he preached Christ.

His theme was, in fact, the making of a Christian — how Saul of Tarsus, Pharisee of the Pharisees, Roman citizen, fanatic opponent of the sect of the Nazarenes became Paul the apostle, the bond servant of Jesus Christ. As usual, Paul had an eye for his audience. So he didn't launch into this theme right away. He didn't blurt out his testimony without regard to his surroundings; nor did he forget he was a prisoner answering a charge. So he began with an elegant flourish, complimenting the king on his knowledge of Jewish customs and then proceeding to a convincing defense of his recent activities. Since it was necessary to explain why he had been the cause of a religious riot in Jerusalem, he slid naturally into an account of his conversion. Before they knew what was happening his regal audience was hearing the story of his encounter with the risen Christ on the Damascus Road.

But he was not allowed to finish. With a roar the Roman governor interrupted. He had had enough of this tale about Moses and the prophets and this Messiah who had risen from the dead. "Paul, you are raving: too much study is driving you mad." "I'm not mad, Your Excellency," said Paul, "what I am saying is sober truth." Then he turned to Agrippa, appealing to his understanding of the Jewish Scriptures: "King Agrippa, do you believe the prophets?" But the king's defenses were up. He knew wnat Paul was after. "You

161

think it will not take much to win me over and make a Christian of me."

The first thing we have to learn about the making of a Christian in any age is that no one — but no one — is excluded from the possibility. If Paul saw in this immoral and cynical rogue the makings of a Christian then his confidence in the Gospel was unbounded. He did so believe for one simple reason. He himself had been, he believed, a much more unlikely candidate for conversion. The conversion of a complete scoundrel is both psychologically and theologically more understandable than the conversion of a deeply religious man of fanatic zeal in the upholding of the moral principles by which he lives. For the scoundrel may well have a festering conscience and be inwardly ready for the volte-face of repentance and faith; but the self-satisfied moralist is sealed against this appeal of the Gospel. In the Gospels it is the rascals and the dissolute who respond rather than the pious. For Paul the conversion of Herod Agrippa would seem in every way a lesser miracle than the conversion of Saul of Tarsus.

Two points emerge for our thinking about the making of Christians today. First, that it should be happening now, as it happened then, by the contagion of belief, the desire to share the experience of Christ. If this story from the Book of the Acts seems in any way remote to us today, it can only be because we have

162

lost this inner dynamic of the Gospel. For centuries there has been a comfortable assumption on the part of Church members that Christians are just made by an automatic process working through heredity and environment. Christians were made, so to speak, by an assembly line provided by the Church. So the impulse to win others to the faith has died away. At the same time modern Christians have felt a reluctance to intrude on the religious life of others. How many of us could really say about our non-Christian contemporaries: "I wish to God that you might become what I am"? It sounds arrogant in our ears. Yet all he is saying is: "I wish to God you were a Christian too." For he is perfectly aware that the objective is not to commend ourselves. "Apart from these chains." We have our chains too. What matters is simply the desire to share our experience of Christ.

Do we truly realize that in the 1970's there is little left of this so-called assembly line? There is no pressure in society today as we know it that is steadily directed towards the making of Christians. Therefore, the Church will surely decline unless again there is an infection of belief, a sincere desire on the part of those who call themselves Christians to communicate their faith. When D. T. Niles was conducting a Christian mission at Edinburgh University, I remember his calling a meeting of believers and asking us: "How many of you have non-Christian friends?" Everyone raised his hand — inwardly perhaps rather proud of the number of atheists and agnostics in his circle. Then he looked at us and said: "Do you ever feel sad about them?"

The other point this story drives home is this question of the raw material from which a Christian is made. Do we really believe that *anyone* without exception can be made a Christian? I know there are many here who do have a desire to communicate the faith. And you are concerned about the outreach of this church. But I find that when we discuss these matters it tends to be taken for granted that only a fraction of those living around us here can be considered potential members of the Church of Christ. I'm not thinking now of those who are members of some other communion. It's not our job to proselytize. I'm thinking of the thousands in this city for whom all religion is irrelevant and the Gospel an unknown factor. Have we virtually written them off? When you think about the friends you might invite to worship with you here, are there not some you automatically rule out? "No use asking him. No use suggesting it to her. They're not the type." *What* type? Is it not time in our new situation of mission to break down this club-psychology by which we set up criteria that have nothing to do with the Gospel? Listen to the clear voice of the New Testament: there is no one at all, anywhere, who is not a potential Christian.

What makes a Christian — today as in these early

times? If you are thinking that so far we have been concentrating on what you might call dramatic conversion — whether of Saul of Tarsus, King Agrippa or your pagan friend — then let me ask just how you and I are made Christians. For most of us there was nothing dramatic about it. But there has been, somewhere along the line, the contagion of another, the desire, the prayer that this should happen to us. Every time parents stand here offering a child for baptism they are, in fact, saying: "I confess that I am a Christian, and I wish to God that this little fellow will be like me — apart from these chains!" In other words, our Christian making — for a great many here — began with the desire of our parents that we should follow them in the Christian way — and do better.

Then other factors come into play. We meet men and women whose influence challenges us and shapes us. We are exposed to the process of Christian education — at home or in church. We are nourished in worship and the receiving of the sacrament. We are moved by books we read, music we hear, plays we see. Perhaps we are shocked into a new awareness of Christ by an experience of great danger, or profound sorrow, or great happiness, or the call to help the starving, the sick in mind and body, the victims of an unjust society. Everyone here could tell a different story about the factors that have been operative in making us Christians. Since there is no standard pattern we are called to accept one another in the faith without questioning the validity of an experience that is quite different from ours.

What is it, then, that gives this word a meaning? If it is not to be limited to those who undergo an upheaval like Saul of Tarsus, then what constitutes a Christian? I would say without hesitation, at the risk of being called a "pietist," a personal loyalty to Jesus Christ. No process, no influence, no ceremony can make me a Christian unless at some point by an act of will I relate myself to Christ as Lord. That is why the only condition of membership in this Church is the willingness to say: "Jesus Christ is my Lord and Savior." The making of a Christian today depends on an encounter with Jesus Christ in which we make a personal and positive response, which may be anything from: "Lord, I believe: help thou mine unbelief," to "My Lord and my God."

But there is something more that has to be said. It is not, in the end, even our personal response that makes us Christians. For this is not something that we do. It is the Spirit of Christ who does the making. "Come after me," he said to his first disciples, "and I will make you fishers of men." Yes; he wants us all to have that desire to win others to his service. But "I will make you" has wider implications. Just as we are constantly exposed to influences today that seek to make us anything from computer fodder to conspicuous consumers, so we are here exposed in the community of the Church to the Spirit that seeks to make us Christians. Anything that interferes with that process has no place among us. Here we know the grace of the Lord Jesus Christ, the love of God and the fellowship of the Holy Spirit; and in worship, friendship and common service we are exposed to the process of being made Christians.

For it is a process. A church is not a club of people who once upon a time had a religious experience and then signed up to live on the memory. It is a community of those who are on the way. And its life will be demonstrated by the constant changes in our opinions, our prejudices, our moral habits, our characters, as we are being made over in the image of Christ. "You think it will not take much to make a Christian of me?" It takes the constant presence of the risen Christ; the daily realization of the overwhelming love of God; and the indwelling and empowering of his Holy Spirit. And as we look ahead into the uncertainties of our mortal days and the certainty that they will come to an end, it is good to know that the making of a Christian never ends.

16

Who Needs God?

The centurion answered and said, Lord, I am not worthy that thou shouldest come under my roof: but speak the word only, and my servant shall be healed.

ST. MATTHEW 8:8

How real a factor is the thought of God in the everyday life of Mr. and Mrs. John Q. Citizen? We know that, when stopped in the street and asked if they believe in God, a surprising 97% say "Yes." But how many honestly could confess to a desperate need of God and say with the psalmist: "As the hart panteth after the water brooks, so panteth my soul after thee, O God"? If there's any kind of panting going on around us it's after power, money or sex rather than God. How many consciously commit each day to God and are aware of his guidance? How many deliberately try to find out the will of God as they make plans for the future? How many regulate their behavior by the thought that there is a God "unto whom all hearts are open, all desires known, and from whom no secrets are hid"? And how many live daily with the thought that there is a presence of God in which we shall find ourselves when these earthly days are over?

Only God knows the answer to these questions. But, from what I know of my own difficulties — as one, you might say, professionally exposed to the thought of God — and from what I hear from others, my guess is that for many God is peripheral rather than central in their lives. If our felt need of him becomes intermittent, our reference to him increasingly rare, then it is not a big step to living entirely without him. And this is surely what has happened to thousands who would hesitate to describe themselves as atheists. God is no longer real. Though they might not say so, they don't really need him. Some have told me, in fact, of their surprise when they found that when they stopped bothering about God, giving up all worship and prayer, life went on much as usual.

It is often said today that this elimination of the thought of God from our daily life is the result of man's new sense of knowledge and control. When we know what makes nature tick, when we are gaining control over her latent forces, when we take round-trips to the moon, when we begin to decide who shall be born, and when we shall die — who needs God? Man has taken over. This kind of reasoning may have affected those for whom God was a kind of backstop for our ignorance, an emergency exit when life was too difficult; but I doubt if anyone who had really known the God and Father of Jesus Christ would ever conclude that he is less real because we have found

169

out a few more of his secrets. Living without God is no modern invention. From the dawn of history men and women have been listening to the whisper in the Garden: "Ye shall be as gods: who needs God?"

This is why I am in revolt against the current mania for adjusting the message of the Church to the supposed mood of the moment in the name of the blessed word, "relevance." Nobody can discuss religion or the Church these days without someone saying: "Yes; but is it relevant?". We are told that the Bible stories in which our fathers delighted are no longer relevant; that the regular services of worship are not relevant in the second half of the twentieth century; and that a sermon is not relevant if it speaks of the grace of God rather than the problems of man. It seems that what matters about a religion today is not its truth but its relevance. So if the mood of the day is interpreted to be "Who needs God?" we are supposed to accept this without question and proceed to talk about something else — provided it is relevant.

Relevant to what? To our immediate needs? Then by this standard an airline schedule is superior to the Sermon on the Mount. Certainly, if I'm in a hotel bedroom in Chicago planning to return to New York, the schedule on the desk is much more relevant to my immediate need than the Gideon Bible in the drawer. In the same way the morning newspaper can be much more relevant than the plays of Shakespeare,

170

and my monthly bank statement than the Mona Lisa.
There could be a moment as I drive along Madison
Avenue when a toot on the horn at a crossing would
be more relevant than all the symphonies of Beethoven.

If by "making the Gospel relevant" is meant express-
ing it in words and actions that ordinary people can
understand, I am all for it. That indeed is what I
hope we are working at together in our church today.
But my conviction is that the Gospel of God's love to
us in Christ is in itself supremely relevant to all men
at all times and in all places. It is not made relevant
by us; and it is not our job to dilute it, or muffle it,
because there are some to whom it does not appeal.
The Bible reveals that *all* men need God, but it is
equally aware that in every age there are many who
don't think they do. We should accept the fact that
for them the Gospel is irrelevant; Christ is irrelevant.
Let's take a few examples.

(1) There are the power-drunk, the men and women
who play God. Listen to the Pharaoh as he receives
in his palace the deputation from his Hebrew slaves.
"Moses and Aaron went in, and told Pharaoh, Thus
saith the Lord God of Israel, Let my people go . . . And
Pharaoh said, Who is the Lord, that I should obey his
voice to let Israel go? I know not the Lord, neither
will I let Israel go." For the ruler of Egypt this talk
of God was rubbish. Do you suppose that as they went
out Moses said to Aaron: "You know, brother, the

171

trouble is our message isn't relevant?". Pharaoh, with what the Bible calls his "hardness of heart," is the symbol of those who are impervious to God-talk, not because it is meaningless, but because they want to be gods themselves. We have had our modern Pharaohs, but the God-men of today are more often the anonymous figures who lurk in the shadows of modern technology, claiming the power to decide the destiny of the human race. Occasionally they surface to declare that man is now the master of his fate and must assume the attributes of God. There is no will in the known universe, they say, but man's will; no authority but man's authority; no moral order but of man's devising. God's prerogative is now man's: "I kill and I make alive." This kind of Titan has no need of God; and for him the Gospel is irrelevant.

(2) This kind of titanism is probably not widespread today, but there is another philosophy of life that excludes God and can be encountered almost every day. I refer to the self-contained and self-satisfied. By this I don't mean the smug, but the man or woman who is prepared to say something like this: "I have my own principles and my standard of judgment; and I am prepared to run under my own steam. I'm neither a saint nor a devil and have no ambitions to be either. My own moral code is quite sufficient for me, and I've no urge to go running to a God for forgiveness or help." You must have come across this attitude among

172

your friends and acquaintances. It amounts to: "I don't need your God; so don't bother me with your Gospel and your Church."

For the self-contained, Christ is irrelevant. He said so: "They that are whole need not a physician; but they that are sick. I came not to call the righteous but sinners to repentance." There are lots of people whom we should never call self-righteous who are, in fact, claiming that there is nothing wrong with them that only a loving God can put right. They are far from being arrogant or self-assertive — they may often be more attractive people than some professing Christians — but their attitude is not fundamentally different from that of the men and women that Jesus couldn't reach. The Pharisees are a much maligned group in the Christian stereotype, but the ones whom our Lord attacked were people who refused his Gospel because they were perfectly satisfied with themselves as they were. So long as we believe that we can run our own lives without outside help then Christ is irrelevant to us. So long as we refuse to admit any moral sickness, anything wrong with our relationships to God or our fellowmen, the Gospel is meaningless. Christ came "to seek and to save that which is lost," and if there is no sense in which we feel spiritually lost, then we don't need this gift of God.

(3) The other type of person who doesn't need God is, of course, the one who has made a god of material

success. For him anything that will help in the acquiring of money or goods is relevant; anything else is not. St. Luke tells us of a man who approached Jesus with a request. "Master, tell my brother to divide the family property with me." Here was our Lord's opportunity to be relevant. And what did he say? "My good man, who set me over you to judge or arbitrate?" Then he said to the crowd: "Beware! Be on your guard against greed of every kind" and went on to tell the story of the man who thought of nothing but material success, expanding his business and assuring an opulent retirement, only to hear the voice that said: "You fool, this very night you must surrender your life; you have made your money — who will get it now?" And his closing words were: "That is how it is with the man who amasses wealth for himself and remains a pauper in the sight of God."

I can imagine that the man who asked for help went away muttering: "I wanted some practical advice, and all I got was a totally irrelevant story." Yet, in fact, the story was the most relevant thing he could have heard. If we decide, in our heart of hearts, that material success, the acquiring of a fortune, is to be our supreme goal, then Christ and his Gospel are irrelevant: we don't need God. We may try to disguise this fact. We may pay lip service to his ideals. We may even try to enlist him as an ally in the making of our fortune. But if we are totally dedicated to material success we don't need God. We have one.

Is there any way in which the Gospel can break through to the power-drunk, the self-satisfied, or the fortune-hunter? It certainly cannot be done by any attempt to adjust the message and make it relevant to their present point of view. Something has to happen. And, as we know from the Bible and from our own experience, time and again it does happen. A man or woman awakens to the need that has been there all the time. Sometimes it is a realization of our ignorance in this vast universe; sometimes it is being suddenly aware of our dependence on the Creator-Spirit; sometimes it is a sense of our ultimate moral weakness in time of strong temptation; sometimes it is a moment of danger; sometimes it is a stab of conscience. The awakening to our need may come gently as in that conversation that Nicodemus had with Christ by night; sometimes it takes an earthquake as with the jailer at Philippi. We then know that we need God. And we are ready to hear the Gospel.

Once in one of our prison camps during World War II, one of my fellow inmates made a rather cynical remark to me. "Have you ever noticed," he asked, "that attendance at church services in the camp varies inversely with the number of Red Cross parcels coming into the camp?" I knew what he meant. When there was a regular distribution of one parcel per man per week, life was roughly normal and church attendance was about what it was at home. But when the parcels slowed down or stopped, we were soon in a kind of crisis situation — and many more began to show up at worship. We've probably noticed the same correlation at work in our society today. A personal or national crisis is apt to make the average citizen begin to think about the God they didn't seem to need before. Who would doubt that a threat of imminent nuclear annihilation would pack the churches right across the land?

I'm not cynical about this sort of thing. Of course, panic religion has no great validity, but there's no harm in waking up to a need that is, in fact, there all the time. In God's eyes we are the sick who need a doctor. The Roman centurion was one who realized this. He could well have been power-drunk. "I say to this man, Go, and he goeth; and to another, Come, and he cometh; and to my servant, Do this, and he doeth it." He could well have been self-satisfied, as a respected officer in an occupied country. He could well have been on the make as a fortune-hunting Roman. But there was in him the essential humility to let him know when he was out of his depth. He loved his servant, and the man was desperately sick. So he was perfectly ready to turn to this native who seemed to possess the healing power of God. "Lord, I am not worthy that thou shouldest come under my roof: but speak the word only, and my servant shall be healed." What

176

humility — and what faith! He just knew he needed God, and believed that Christ could heal.

There is not one of us here who does not live from time to time as though we had no need of God. Much of the society in which we live is based on that assumption. But when we reach the bedrock facts of life and death, there is no one who can easily dismiss the summons of the eternal or despise the grace that is offered us in Christ. There comes the moment of reflection when we know we are not gods, when our self-confidence is shattered, when our material goals turn to dust and ashes. Then we are ready to say: "Lord, I am not worthy... speak the word only, and thy servant shall be healed." And the God we need will be there.

17

Charisma Is a Christian Word

There are varieties of gifts, but the same Spirit. There are varieties of service, but the same Lord.

I CORINTHIANS 12:4,5 (NEB)

A few years ago if I used the word "charisma" in a sermon title only the theologians and Greek scholars in the congregation would have had any idea what I was talking about. Today everyone here must have heard or seen the word, whether or not it registered in your mind. It is one of these words like "viable," "meaningful," "power-structures" or (more recently) "abrasive" that suddenly surfaces from the semantic depths to decorate the prose of columnists, TV commentators, committee reports and "with-it" preachers (although a preacher who uses "with-it" by now is no longer with-it).

"Charisma" has been found a useful word to describe an elusive quality of charm, personal magnetism and persuasive power, the capacity to excite and inspire one's fellowmen. I suppose the word has come into circulation because it is so difficult to find another that adequately describes this human electricity. Two politicans may be equal in ability, experience and ambition: one has charisma and the other hasn't. Two actors may be equally brilliant and talented: one has charisma and the other hasn't. Two society ladies may be equally rich and beautiful: one has charisma and the other hasn't. Two school teachers may be equally competent and well equipped: one has charisma and the other hasn't. Charisma has nothing to do with a sober estimate of achievement or with our personal likes or dislikes. For instance, it would probably be agreed by those who use this word that of the presidents we have known in the last fifty years, Roosevelt, Eisenhower and Kennedy had charisma. Charisma is morally neutral. Gandhi had it—and so had Hitler.

The word can also be used today to describe the mystique of an office. There is said to be a charisma of the presidency that belongs to it and descends upon even the least charismatic of its holders.

It occurred to me that the Bible is filled with characters who had charisma. One book you probably seldom read is the Book of Judges. These "judges" were not the kind we solemnly elect to dispense justice. They were folk heroes, men and women who rose to leadership during the period of turbulence and savagery that preceded the establishment of the Kingdom of Israel. Today we could call "Judges" the "Book of the Charismatics." Think of the odd assortment of mystics, thugs, heroes, saints and savages represented by the names Deborah, Barak, Gideon, Abimelech, Jephthah,

Samson (Samson had everything — physique, brains, self confidence, magnetism and a way with women). These are the people with charisma, how ever it was used. Saul had it and died miserably after a catastrophic defeat in war. David had it and died in a comfortable bed. The supreme example, of course, is in the New Testament. If there had been modern reporters around when Jesus was on his Galilean campaign, the word "charisma" would have been overworked. When .he preached people "were astonished." How could this carpenter whose family were such ordinary people have such power? It was unbelievable that one from his background should be swaying the multitudes. Charisma is, among other things, the quality that makes a crowd long to touch the person who possesses it and to grab any piece of his clothing. You remember the woman who broke through the crowd to touch the hem of his garment?

If we stopped with this picture of charisma as it is drawn for us today, this sermon would take a very different turn. You would expect me to assess its value and moralize about its use. In spite of the general agreement that charisma is just something you have or haven't, that it cannot be acquired, you might even expect me to show you how to get it. (I rejected my first title for this sermon — "Do you have charisma?" chiefly because it sounded like such an offer!) Any day I expect to see an advertisement for a Charisma School, offering a course in twelve easy lessons on the installment plan, but by that time the word will be on its way out, and perhaps some other theological term will have been purloined by the phrase-maker. What I want to do is something very different. Like all others who have been to seminary, I was familiar with the word, charisma, long before any wordhound of today got on its track. The startling fact is that charisma is a Christian word, almost uniquely — like agape — a New Testament word. It is scarcely known in classical Greek but occurs again and again in the writing of the apostles. If you consult a dictionary as recent as the Webster of 1960, you will find no mention of the current use of the word. I have been wondering how many people, having to look this word up in the dictionary in recent days, have been baffled and confused by reading this: "Charisma — an extraordinary power, as of, working miracles, or speaking with tongues, said to be possessed by early Christians." Lots of puzzled people must have been in difficulties trying to apply that to the charismatic figures they are reading about today.

Charisma, in the New Testament, derives from the Greek word, charis, meaning grace. Grace is the little word that contains all we know of the Gospel. Our sense of God's presence — that is grace. His help when we are weak — that is grace. His forgiveness of our sins — that is grace. Grace is the love of God in action; grace is divine healing; grace is suffering transmuted into hope and joy; grace is everything that Christ means to those who know him. A charisma, then, is a gift of God that flows from his grace. It is an endowment of the Spirit, and can take many different forms. "There are varieties of gifts (the word is charisma) but the same Spirit." The Church was known in the earliest days as the community where ordinary men and women were transformed by the Spirit of God, and each one had his own special charisma. The Epistle to the Hebrews says that "God added his testimony by signs, by miracles, by manifold works of power and by distributing the gifts (charisma) of the Holy Spirit at his own will."

St. Paul uses the same word when he says: "The gifts we possess differ as they are allotted to us by God's grace and must be exercised accordingly: the gift of inspired utterance, for example, in proportion to a man's faith; or the gift of administration in administration. A teacher should employ his gift in teaching and one who has the gift of stirring speech should use it to stir his hearers. If you give to charity, give with all your heart; if you are a leader, exert yourself to lead; if you are helping others in distress, do it cheerfully." Even this short list which is supplemented in other epistles gives an idea of how different one person's charisma can be from another's. Prayer, administration, teaching, preaching, charitable giving, leadership, being a friend in need — in the living Church of Christ everyone has his own

182

charisma. "Unto every one of us," we read, "is given grace according to the measure of the gift of Christ."

We're already a long way from the charisma we are hearing about today. Whoever first plucked this word from its New Testament context or filched it from the theologians, probably fastened on to one luminous idea — that of a mysterious quality that defies analysis and exudes the kind of charm which hovers around the word "grace." The charisma of the New Testament and the charisma the journalists are talking about have this in common: it cannot be manufactured or bought for cash.

Charisma is a Christian word. Let me summarize the striking differences between the Christian meaning and its popular use today.

(1) *The Christian charisma is not the possession of a small élite: it is given to all who believe.* We can all think of outstanding Christian leaders like Schweitzer, Pope John, Martin Luther King, who had charisma in the popular sense; but the New Testament says that such leadership is only one kind of charisma. Equally important is the gift of prayer, of making friends, of organizing, of supplying funds for missions, of visiting the sick, of teaching the young, of the helping hand. The most dynamic preacher in the pulpit has no more charisma in the Christian sense than a member in the workroom sewing for the hospitals or an usher with the gift of welcoming visitors. Singing in the choir, teaching an

immigrant English, standing by an alcoholic, preparing a budget, breaking down barriers of race or color or age — all can be charisma. "There are varieties of gifts, but the same Spirit." For too long we have associated the Spirit only with the more spectacular gifts. God is telling us that every single one of us who looks to Christ as Lord has a charisma. A healthy church is not one which relies on a small group of people who have some kind of charisma in the modern sense, but one which unites a great diversity of charisma in the fellowship of the Spirit. "There are varieties of service, but the same Lord." The housebound or bedridden church member who exercises the charisma of prayer, sometimes too the offering of pain and distress in union with the Crucified, is as active in the church as the busiest committee chairman, and the gifted committee chairman has as much Christian charisma as the most electrifying visiting preacher. If you are a Christian you have your charisma. Perhaps what we need is the word of St. Paul to Timothy: "I now remind you to stir into flame the gift of God which is within you." When I am asked: "What is your goal for this church?" a good answer would be: "A community in which every member has stirred into flame the charisma God has given — whatever it is." For "there are varieties of gifts, but the same Spirit. There are varieties of service, but the same Lord."

(2) The second line that divides the Christian charisma from the popular word today is this: *charisma in*

the New Testament is the gift of the Spirit of Christ and is, therefore, exercised solely in the service of others. Thus the Christian rules out the notion of a charisma that is used to dominate and control, the charisma that is self-serving and self-glorifying. Here is the Christian charisma in action: "If then our common life in Christ yields anything to stir the heart, any loving consolation, any sharing of the Spirit, any warmth or affection or compassion, fill my cup of happiness by thinking and feeling alike, with the same love for one another, the same turn of mind, a common care for unity. Rivalry and personal vanity should have no place among you, but you should humbly reckon others better than your-selves. You must look to each other's interest and not merely to your own. Let your bearing towards one an-other arise out of your life in Christ Jesus."

St. Paul knew the subtle temptation to make even Christian gifts minister to self-glorification. There were some in these young churches, for instance, who rejoiced in the gift of tongues. The apostle acknowledged this as a charisma, but what he told them was: "Unless your gift ministers to building up of the church — shut up!" "Thank God," were his words, "I am more gifted in ecstatic utterance than any of you, but in the congrega-tion I would rather speak five intelligible words, for the benefit of others as well as myslf, than thousands of words in the language of ecstasy." This is not our par-ticular problem, but do we always escape the peril of self-service in the name of religious devotion?

As Jesus was "the man for others," so his gifts are not for our self-satisfaction but for the service of others. If anyone comes knocking at the door of the Christian Charisma School seeking a spiritual power to attract others to himself, or a peace and calm of mind for his own satisfaction, he will find that this door swings open on a world where his brothers are starving, wounded, lonely, hopeless, crippled and a Voice will say: "Take my charisma: heal the sick, cleanse the lepers, raise the dead, feed the hungry, visit the lonely, cast out devils."

(3) And the third dividing line is this: *unlike this modern charisma which just seems to happen where the lightning strikes, Christian charisma is a gift to be sought and found, and a gift that grows.* The most wonderful experience in a living church is not the emergence of outstanding personalities who attract attention, but the transformation of ordinary people by the Spirit of Christ. Our purpose here, according to our accepted Statement, is "to bring men and women into the transforming presence of Christ, in the fellowship of the Spirit, that they may be made over in his likeness." Is that happening to you and me? Or have we ceased to hope for this spiritual power that takes the gifts we have and makes them glow with Christian charisma in the service of our fellowmen?

We will always need leaders with what our world calls charisma, and we pray that they will be men of integrity and faith. But even more do we need, injected into our divided and anguished world, a company of men and women who seek from God the charisma of Christlike living. This, more than anything else, is the function of the Church. In God's eyes it is not the charm and dazzle of a magnetic personality that counts. It is the desire of any one of his family to have and to use the charisma he is waiting to bestow. Have we really listened to these words of Jesus: "Is there a father among you who will offer his son a snake when he asks for a fish, or a scorpion when he asks for an egg? If you, then, bad as you are, know how to give your children what is good for them, how much more will the heavenly Father give the Holy Spirit to those who ask him?"

18

Signposts of the Spirit

Marvel not that I said unto thee, Ye must be born again.

ST. JOHN 3:7

We are now learning to live with the thought that man is launched into new territories of space. No one knows where this adventure will lead or what inconceivable discoveries await the coming generation. If there is a noticeable restraint in our celebration of this giant stride beyond the orbit of the earth, this new vista on the universe, the reason is obvious. We are not at all sure that man is spiritually equal to the challenge, morally mature enough to exploit new territory and new powers for good and not for evil. We would like to think that the space platforms of the future would be science's gift to the benefactors of the human race. We fear that they may fall into the hands of the malefactors — that, in fact, a lethal instrument is being offered to a juvenile delinquent. For the present atmosphere of high tension, with flaming incitements to racial hatreds and religious bigotry in every corner of the world, is not exactly reassuring.

Yet, there are some signs on the horizon that offer hope. The very fact that we are so aware of the terrifying gap between our technical prowess and our spiritual resources indicates that man may be now ready for the inward exploration that is overdue. As compared with fifty years ago there is little confidence now that human reason alone can direct our new skills into fruitful and peaceful channels. There must be few left who believe that science can provide its own answers to the ethical questions that have been sharpened for us by its achievements. In many quarters today there is a new search into that realm of values which was neglected while we concentrated on the exploration and control of the physical universe. The hunt is on for insights into other levels of consciousness. We are not so sure any more that reason is the sole legitimate arbiter of human destiny or that the physical sciences alone tell us the truth about our human condition. Religion, psychiatry, art and ethics are moving to the center of attention as the inward exploration proceeds. This may often have little to do with conventional church activity as we have known it, but who can doubt that millions are now looking for what I am calling "signposts of the Spirit"?

It is in this context that I want to listen again to the recorded conversation between Christ and Nicodemus, and to hear the haunting words: "Ye must be born again." Whatever else preachers and theologians have

found in this passage there can be no question that it
deals with this inner life, this discovery of the invisible
world, this renewal of spiritual awareness. In Biblical
language the theme is the Kingdom of God. Nicodemus
is here the wise man, the moral man, the religious man
— from other references in the Gospels also a man of
courage and integrity. Yet apparently he has not gotten
to first base in this matter of the Kingdom. Like most
of us he has been trained to approach God through
mental channels, to learn his religion through a set of
principles and to practice it reasonably and sensibly in
his daily life. There's nothing wrong with that. Jesus
never condemned the use of the mind and obedience to
moral principles. On the contrary he stressed that we
should love the Lord our God "with all our mind," and
he loved the young man who professed to have faith-
fully kept the commandments. But he always suggested
that there was something missing. "One thing thou
lackest." The secret of the Kingdom lay elsewhere.

Here speaks the courteous and respected religious
scholar: "Rabbi, we know that thou art a teacher come
from God: for no man can do these miracles that thou
doest, except God be with him." Sensible, practical,
rational — the kind of opening that seems to demand
an equally rational reply. Yet what is the response of
Jesus? A totally abrupt and enigmatic pronouncement,
delivered with the emphasis he always reserved for his
most decisive teaching. "Verily, verily I say unto thee,

Except a man be born again, he cannot see the kingdom of God." Nicodemus is left floundering as he tries to make literal sense of what he has heard. "How can a man be born when he is old? can he enter the second time into his mother's womb, and be born?" Again, Jesus returns to his theme. "Except a man be born of water and of the Spirit, he cannot enter into the kingdom of God. That which is born of the flesh is flesh; and that which is born of the Spirit is spirit. Marvel not that I said unto *thee, Ye* must be born again." (The switch to the plural expands the conversation to include us all.)

What does it mean? Whether we translate "born again," or "born from above," the demand is for an inner revolution, a spiritual rebirth. The accepted teaching was that the Kingdom was to be reached by meticulous observance of the law, by correct thoughts and good works. Religion was the crowning achievement of the mature man, and the Kingdom was the reward of true piety. Now Christ is dismissing the conventional apparatus of religion and saying that the secret of the Kingdom lies elsewhere. He is forcing us to face the possibility that we have built up layers of religious ideas and practices that have smothered the simple response, the primitive intuition, the spontaneous wonder that belongs to the child within. Exactly the same thought is expressed in the words: "Except ye be converted, and become as little children, ye shall not enter into the kingdom of heaven."

This is not a plea for what people sometimes call "simple faith," meaning a sentimental attachment to childish images and a refusal to rethink one's beliefs in the light of new knowledge and experience. To be reborn, to become as a little child is the process by which anyone from the simplest to the most sophisticated enters that new level of consciousness in which the world of spirit becomes intensely real. A man can have the genius of an Einstein or a Schweitzer and still enter this Kingdom as a little child. In the huge variety of temperament and ability we find in the men and women known to the Church as "saints," the one common feature is precisely this rebirth by which they knew God with the simplicity and spontaneity of a child. What is demanded is not a renunciation of the intellect or the repudiation of mature experience, but an enlargement of our capacity to respond to the unseen world, the gift of the pure in heart who see God. What has to be stripped away is the surface sophistication, the confidence that we can think our way into ultimate truth and the arrogance of our supposed maturity.

It is the freshness, the imagination, the insight of the child within, that has to be rediscovered — not the tantrums and the self pity. In our rebirth we find again the wonder of the child gazing through a window at the moon, the imagination of the child who sees a palace in an empty can, the insight of the child who knows that God is laughing with him as he bounces on his bed, the freedom of the child who really believes that "this is my Father's world." It is this child within us who is struggling to be reborn, and whom we tether by our "adultery." (Not a bad word to use, you know, since we are talking about a way of being faithless to our God.)

So the child within is a signpost of the Spirit, pointing to neglected avenues of the soul, to areas of awareness long forgotten. Surely the artist knows this signpost as he expresses in paint, in music or in words what cannot be reduced to the logic of common sense. We are also beginning to understand the importance of the primitive instincts of the human race. No longer are they merely material for anthropology. The childhood of humanity is alive, and when we listen to it new doors are opened into the world of spirit. For centuries educated Christians were embarrassed by the dreams and symbols of the Bible. Now we are beginning to understand how dreams are often our contact with the childhood of the race and offer clues to the inner world where the impossible is acceptable and two and two make five. In a very real sense "we are such stuff as dreams are made of", and here again "a little child shall lead us" into new levels of consciousness.

The way to rebirth is marked by many symbols. They are indeed the signposts of the Spirit. A symbol is a physical object, very much in this material world, that opens a door into the world invisible. The Stars and Stripes is a piece of colored cloth that can be sold for a few cents. But it can be the door to a range of emotions that lie deep in the soul. A daisy may be one of millions in a meadow, yet one between our fingers may suddenly light the way into the mystery. Listen to Tennyson:

> "Flower in the crannied wall,
> I pluck you out of the crannies; —
> Hold you here, root and all, in my hand,
> Little flower — but if I could understand
> What you are, root and all, and all in all,
> I should know what God and man is."

Who has not known the moment when the ordinary suddenly became the extraordinary, and some simple object, the flaming signpost of the world unseen? As I was preparing this sermon among my mail was a letter from a Radio Pulpit listener enclosing a poem. Sometimes my heart sinks when this happens, but a glance at the page made me read on and wonder why just this letter should have come my way that morning. For here is someone describing exactly the kind of experience I am struggling to express:

> "In mid-lake, I weigh anchor and rest on the oars
> To watch the baptismal rites at the water's edge.

The demented cry of a loon drifts from the far reeds;
Then the sun steps into the lake, and a sheet of gold
                                                    ablaze:
Fire trembles and burns and my boat and I are reborn,
Gone all rational thought, and the visceral nerve
Eats and drinks the flesh and blood in the age-old thirst
To be caught and held in the glory of God
Past all undoing, to the last drawn earthly breath."

"Ye must be born again." To reach the inner Kingdom, to be more sure of God, to draw strength from a
source beyond the human horizons, to know the place
where Christ is waiting with new life streaming from
the hands that were pierced, we need more than words
and phrases, more than the routines of religion. We
need the symbols that expand our consciousness, and
open up those cobwebbed avenues where the child
once walked. We need that water that comes from an
ordinary tap, but here in church is the baptismal sign
of rebirth "of water and of the Spirit." And we need
in our worship also the moment when words like mine
now fall silent and the symbol becomes the signpost of
the Spirit.

Sermon and sacrament belong together in our tradition. The Reformers knew how symbols without understanding can be superstition, and mystery can become
magic. But they also knew that there is truth that passes all understanding, and mystery that cannot be

contained in words. So here we let these material elements be the signposts of the Spirit, and our eating and drinking be our communion with the unseen Christ. So we become more conscious of that most real world within from which alone we can gain strength to meet the moral crises of our day. To be a Christian is continually to begin all over again, to let the child awaken, to let the symbols speak. The Sacrament of Christ's body and blood is the nourishment of the reborn and the pledge of life eternal.

19
Virtue and Vice

". . . a good tree always yields good fruit, and a poor tree bad fruit."

ST. MATTHEW 7:17 (NEB)

A cabinet minister in England recently made the remark that children in school today were wasting their time learning about the Wars of the Roses when they should be absorbing all the facts about Vietnam. Leaving aside the absurdity of supposing that anyone at all could learn all the facts about Vietnam, I find this point of view as foolish as it is familiar. It is a belated echo of the late Henry Ford's dictum that history is bunk. It's easy to pour scorn on those who know more about "battles long ago" than the politics on our doorstep, but this is hardly our problem today. We are obsessed by the notion that we are a generation out on our own. The train has accelerated, the coupling has broken and the coaches of the past can be left back there to gather dust. We demand leaders who are immersed in the problems of the 1970's and seldom ask if they are informed about the nation's past. Books are written on social and religious questions with scarcely a glance back to the experience of our ancestors, and snap judgments made without the slightest

197

historical perspective. Seminarians tell me that hours spent in wrestling with immediate concerns of modern society are worth more than the study of Augustine, Calvin or Luther. Everybody is dancing on the hotplate of modernity, as if there were no steadying ancestral blood running in our veins. Yet, something tells me that when it comes to a life-and-death decision in these days of nuclear power, I would rather have, with his finger on the trigger, a man who knew a little about the Wars of the Roses than one who knew all about the latest sociology and physics.

The testing ground is ethics. Behind every other debate that rages now — whether it's about nuclear weapons, hunger, birth control, race relations, education or the family — lies the question of what is good and what is bad. Listen to any protagonist looming up on our TV screens and you'll hear him say: "For me it's a moral issue." Suddenly it seems, modern man has realized that morality doesn't just take care of itself, that it is not delivered as a by-product of technological progress. Surely it is also dawning on us that ethics do not evolve like the physical sciences so that today's theories make the old ones obsolete. Can anyone point to a new ethical discovery that makes the demand to love our neighbor as ourselves old-fashioned and invalid? It makes no more sense to dismiss the moral codes of the past than to ignore Rembrandt and Shakespeare because we now have Picasso and Arthur Miller.

198

Virtue And Vice

Now it happens that a considerable body of ethics has come down to us, and until recently it was accepted in at least the Western world as practically axiomatic. You might transgress the code, but you didn't argue about it any more than you argued about the multiplication table even though you sometimes got your sums wrong. These moral rules came to us from Judaism, from the Greeks and from Christ. There were virtues — honesty, generosity, courage, kindness, chastity, faith, hope, charity. There were vices — lying, cheating, greed, promiscuity, jealousy, pride, aggressiveness and the like. For centuries almost every great work of art reflected man's moral struggle among these virtues and vices for nearly everyone accepted the distinction. When Hamlet reproached his mother for adultery and complicity in murder, there was no debate about "situation ethics" and the validity of his judgment. "Assume a virtue if you have it not," he says, speaking for an age in which vice paid that tribute to virtue that has been called hypocrisy. In the eighteenth century Dr. Johnson denounced a moral relativist with one of his cannonades of common sense. "If he really does think that there is no distinction between virtue and vice, why, Sir, when he leaves our houses let us count our spoons."

What has happened to this moral backbone of society, this framework of virtues and vices? Hardly anyone even likes to use such words today. If we talk about virtues we are said to be moralistic, and if we call any-

199

thing a vice we are judgmental. The word "good" is contaminated by its association with "goody-goody" and "do-gooder" while the word "bad" is just as taboo. The most you can say is "anti-social," and a "bad boy" becomes a "juvenile delinquent." All this is symptomatic of a flight from the inherited code — a flight that began as a necessary corrective but has now become a panic. Every moral judgment is now dotted with question-marks, and we are all involved in ethical dilemmas, at home and in business which would have startled our forefathers. "How do I know what is right?" is the most frequent question of those who care, while many are content to drift along on a tide of popular hedonism — "if it suits me, or gives me kicks, to hell with ethics." Few modern dramas or novels take seriously the moral distinctions that were real to the classics. The Greeks were anything but mealy-mouthed, but their tragedies dealt with profound questions of good and evil. Chaucer may be bawdy, as the theatre notices delight to inform us, but he was dealing with virtues and vices, openly seen for what they were. In contrast, so many modern works either ignore them entirely or deliberately exalt vice as the chief end of man.

I am talking of the moral chaos of our times, not the moral depravity. In spite of best sellers in print or on film, there is no reason to suppose that the average citizen today is any more immoral than in any other age. The younger generation at the moment seems more concerned with ethics than almost anything else. And the average man is certainly more sensitive to questions of justice, racial prejudice and equal opportunity than he was fifty years ago. What we have now is not so much immorality on a new scale as a growing *a*morality, a state of confusion and skepticism about the ethical traditions in which we were raised. When there is no longer a strong, or even a lurking, conviction that virtues are anchored in the will of an eternal God and vices are a defiance of the moral order, then it is not surprising that the lines are blurred, and the Christian standards give way to the new hedonism of a "playboy philosophy." In recent years the churches seem often to have added to the confusion by leaning over backwards to meet the relativism of the age and exploiting the love "that covers a multitude of sins."

If this begins to sound like one of these appeals to "return to the standards of our fathers," as if all we had to do was to re-issue a list of virtues and vices and demand acceptance, then I'm off the track. For authentic Christianity and its message is something very different from the admonition: "Be virtuous and you'll be rewarded in heaven; be vicious and you'll be punished in hell." We are not the first generation to discover that dangers lie in any religion of external morality. It was Christ himself who exposed the weakness of the virtuous and revealed the potential of the vicious. And since his day there have been many exposures of the pretensions of the self-consciously virtuous.

The morality of "virtues and vices" is open to attack on many fronts. It can produce the self-righteousness of the man who thanks God he is not like other men and has no compassion for the frailties of human nature. It can make a man grim and censorious like the Puritan Malvolio to whom Sir Toby Belch addressed the immortal reproach: "Dost thou think because thou art virtuous, there shall be no more cakes and ale?". Above all it may breed the hypocrisy that keeps the letter of the law in outward behavior while all kinds of vice festers within. Christ and his apostles delivered a far more devastating attack on the perversions of this kind of moralism than any of our modern critics. The Gospel allows for no ultimately virtuous man. "There is none good but God." "I am not come to call the righteous but sinners to repentance." "While we were yet sinners, Christ died for us." "By grace are ye saved through faith; and that not of yourselves: it is the gift of God: Not of works, lest any man should boast." The Christian has no virtues to boast of.

Christian morality, then is not the slavish following of a book of rules, and most certainly not the uncritical acceptance of the conventions of any particular age, whether that of the Pilgrims or the Victorians. It depends rather on rebirth in the Spirit. It is not a matter of straining to achieve virtues and avoid vices but of allowing the Spirit of Christ to work within so that the qualities we value may appear with the natural inevitability of leaves on a healthy tree. "A good tree always yields good fruit," said Jesus, "and a poor tree bad fruit." It was exactly the same thought that St. Paul expressed when he said: "Let the Spirit direct your lives, and do not satisfy the desires of the human nature . . . the Spirit produces love, joy, peace, patience, kindness, goodness, faithfulness, humility, and self-control." These are "the harvest of the Spirit"—not the proud achievement of the virtuous man. And you will notice that these listed virtues are somewhat different from those of the so-called conventional code of respectability. They all come from within.

But this morality of the Gospel — we're none of us good and our hope is in the new life that Christ works within us — can be twisted into an immorality that denies the validity of our ideas of right and wrong, virtue and vice. St. Paul in this letter is with one hand proclaiming the freedom of the Christian from living by the letter of the law, but with the other he is warning against flinging the moral code to the winds. Tell a man that he is not saved by being virtuous but by receiving the grace of God, and he may conclude that he is free to cut loose among all the vices he has secretly yearned for. That is why the apostle says: "You were called to be free. But do not let this freedom become an excuse for letting your physical desires rule you." And elsewhere he wrote: "Shall we continue in sin, that grace may abound? God forbid."

When I ask for a new look at virtue and vice, then, I am not suggesting a return to some stern Puritan moralism of the past, but I am protesting against the kind of "situation ethics" that, in the name of Christian love, flings every moral code out of the window. In the present morass of amorality I doubt the wisdom of broadcasting Augustine's summary of Christian ethics: "Love God — and do what you like." Taken seriously it is profoundly true, for to love God is to have the roots of the good tree that will produce the good fruit. But is this the moment — when the very word "God" is called in question by theologians and "loving God" is a meaningless expression to millions, for the churches to shout about "doing what you like"? St. Paul, the archapostle of Christian freedom, didn't mince his words when he came to vices. This is how he described the human nature that has to be tamed by the Spirit. "Immoral, filthy, and indecent actions; worship of idols and witchcraft. People become enemies, they fight, become jealous, angry, and ambitious. They separate into parties and groups; they are envious, get drunk, have orgies, and do other things like these. I warn you now as I have before: those who do these things will

204

not receive the Kingdom of God." Would it do us
any harm, if any of these things seem familiar, to stop
calling them by fancy names or accepting them as
normal and natural, and see them for what they are —
just vices?

And is virtue such an ugly word? I'm tired of the
caricatures of the decent citizen that fill our novels
and plays and movies — as if the only happy man is
the hell-raiser, the only fulfilled woman the one who
sleeps around. I'm even more tired of the accentuation
of the abnormal, the exaltation of the vicious, the assumption that everything history has called virtuous
is mere hypocrisy and fraud. "The Spirit produces love,
joy, peace" — do we not value these in our strident
society where the voices of hatred and violence get
louder? "The Spirit produces patience, kindness, goodness" — could our homes, our offices, our schools, our
streets not use a little more of these? "The Spirit produces faithfulness, humility, and self-control" — do we
think that we are better off with our tale of broken
vows, pride, and permissiveness?

No one who enlists in the cause of Christ today or
accepts service in his Church is setting up to be better
than his neighbor or as a loveless critic of society. As a
Christian, I don't want to be "holier than thou;" but I
want to be holier than I am. We come to worship;
we say our prayers; we respond to the Word of God so
that the Spirit of Christ may work within us, purging

the vices and making us the kind of people in whom these virtues are spontaneous, natural and totally unconscious. At a time when the external moral codes are crumbling, it is more than ever necessary for the Church to be a community where we learn the inner disciplines of the Spirit.

20

Religion Without Wrappings

For there is nothing covered, that shall not be revealed;
neither hid, that shall not be known.

ST. LUKE 12:2

This text came floating into my mind recently in circumstances not even remotely connected with preaching a sermon or devout meditation. I was wrestling with one of those cellophane-wrapped, hermetically-sealed packages of bacon. The stuff was there all right, but could I get at it? The genius who had wrapped and sealed that bacon must have not only invented an impenetrable plastic but perfected a sealing operation designed for eternity. At such a moment — especially if the frying pan is already smoking with expectation — it is good to know that "there is nothing covered that shall not be revealed." And sure enough, I discovered that by bringing a fork sharply down from a great height an initial penetration can be made which can be subsequently skillfully enlarged.

Wrappings. Naturally, I've been thinking about them; for this may go down in history as the age of packaging. No people have ever had their foodstuffs, their literature, their cosmetics, their philosophy, their politics and their religion served up to them so sedulously wrapped. There must be millions who are employed, not in producing goods or ideas, but in wrapping them up. That goes for everything from bacon to theology. Bringing home the bacon is not the simple operation it was when the caveman went hunting; and bringing home the theology now involves distilling Tillich and Bultmann into bright paperbacks and snappy slogans about the "death of God." Don't imagine I am against *all* packaging. Convenience and hygiene dictate its necessity. The question is whether we have reached the point of confusing the package with the contents or of preferring to live with the wrappings to the reality inside.

The purpose of a wrapping, I suppose, is to preserve and keep clean, as well as to attract. And nothing worthwhile can endure without packaging of some kind. The Egyptian mummies are perhaps the supreme example of really efficient wrapping, and we owe a lot to the unknown men who carefully sealed the Dead Sea Scrolls into jars. The invention of printing was a triumph of packaging for it meant that a huge store of human wisdom could be sealed and delivered to millions who would otherwise have remained in ignorance. The great institutions of mankind — congress, parliament, courts of law, universities, museums, trade unions, charitable organizations — serve as wrappings for the enduring principles by which civilization lives, and those who attack them in the name of radical revolution are liable to discover that without some great wrappings of this kind we shall soon be back in the jungle. So it is with the Church. In one sense it is nothing more than the wrapping in which the Gospel comes to us. But without this wrapping which of us here would ever have received the Gospel? Those who would tear it away, getting rid of the whole complex of churches, rituals, creeds, councils and committees in the name of private religion or a spontaneous community have to ask themselves how the Gospel will be preserved, and who will keep it clean. Jesus knew what he was doing when he transformed the personal confession of Simon Peter into the foundation of a new community: "Thou art Peter, and upon this rock I will build my church." This wrapping for the Gospel, as we shall note, has not always been the perfect preserver, nor has it always kept the Gospel clean. But without the worship, the witness, the instruments and officers of the Church there can be no continuing Christianity, nor would any of us here today have ever heard the Gospel.

Now, let me swing back to my worries in this age of packaging. Granted its necessity, we have to look critically at some of the forms it takes today, especially as it applies to religion both personal and corporate.

(1). The return to the *impenetrable* wrapping with which I began: what kind of impression are our churches making on people who have a religious hunger today? Don't you think that the message of Christ has often been sealed off from our contemporaries by the wrappings of the organization? We have covered what should be revealed and hid what should be known. There's something impenetrable to the person who was not raised within the surface machinery of a church like ours. It *is* difficult for a stranger to penetrate the jungle of our organizations, officials, programs and literature, and find out what we are trying to say and to do. It *can* be hard to penetrate our forms of worship to find the living center of our faith. There is a growing resistance today to these wrappings of religion. For one person I meet who is an avowed unbeliever, I meet ten who are what you might call "open to Christ" but closed to the forms in which we seem to have wrapped him. This is why a living church must continually look to its structures of life and worship and be ready for change. But we must remember also that merely changing the wrappings will not guarantee that the Gospel will shine through. There is a modern jargon that is just as impenetrable as the platitudes of the past, and Christ can be obscured by some kind of "swinging liturgy" just as effectively as in the trappings of conventional worship.

210

What matters is the breakthrough of the *real* — the real Gospel, the real Christ, the real you and me. When the Spirit is really present, and when church members are their real selves — and not wearing the masks of religious convention — then it is not hard for anyone to penetrate the wrappings and know what it is all about. Let me illustrate what I mean. A friend of mine asked his confirmation class to compose a prayer in their own language. The next week they began to read them. The first one started off: "We beseech thee, almighty God . . ." "Just a minute," said the minister, "is that really how you talk?" "No." "Then," he said, "tell me in your own words just what your biggest worry is." He thought a moment. "I suppose it's my parents being on my back all the time. That's my hang-up." "Then why don't you tell God that?" "But you can't say *that* in church!" There we have it. "You can't say *that* in church!" So long as we feel that certain normal things are unmentionable in church and that God can only be formally addressed in vague generalities we're not being real.

The trouble begins, then, with the wrappings within which we have enclosed our own selves and our real problems and real beliefs. Sometimes a man will settle for a conventional belief at an early age, lodge it somewhere within and then wrap it and seal it for eternity. He doesn't want to examine it again. He doesn't want any questions raised and is not prepared to open his heart on these matters to anyone at all. Or a woman may think of her religion as a precious heirloom that must never be exposed to the gaze of anyone else. One way or another most of us have been like the man in the parable who said to his Lord: "I was afraid, and went and hid thy talent in the earth." "But there is nothing covered that shall not be revealed; neither hid that shall not be known," and the sooner we are honest with ourselves, and with our neighbors and with God the better. New life comes to the individual and to a church as we learn to remove the wrappings and be ourselves — so that Christ can be *himself* with his healing power. Or it may be that life itself will deal us the blow, like the descending fork, that opens up the package.

(2). But there's another kind of package. Let me say a word about the *unnecessary* wrapping.

I can't help thinking now of the fate of the man who buys a new shirt. All I want is a simple cover that has kept it clean. What I am faced with is a monstrous contraption with the scales of an armadillo and the quills of a porcupine in a forest of cardboard and tissue paper. Another parable. The Church has been guilty of hiding the Gospel by elaborating the unnecessary. One section will insist on the necessity of correct ritual, the importance of vestments, genuflections and candles. Another will offer the Gospel only if you are prepared to accept a whole catalogue of beliefs from the historicity of Adam and Eve to the literal acceptance of the visions of the Revelation. Another will frown on anyone who dares to follow Christ without accepting their taboos on smoking, drinking and dancing. Another wraps the Gospel in a huge blanket of social activity and administrative business and says that you must become "involved." Another identifies the Gospel with a particular political viewpoint, right or left, and virtually excommunicates those who do not toe the line.

It seems to me that our Lord spent much of his time liberating people from these unnecessary wrappings. The freedom that he brought was the ability to cut loose from the things that clog our access to the Father and to concentrate on the essentials. It was this he had in mind when he said: "Come unto me, all ye that labour and are heavy laden, and I will give you rest." The context shows that the "weary and heavy laden" are those who are bowed down with unnecessary religious and moral baggage. There is probably no one here who has not, from time to time, carried excess luggage of this kind. What a relief it is to be done with it and to realize that many beliefs and practices that used to seem important can really be labeled "Not wanted on the voyage." To know Christ as Lord and Savior, to seek to obey him and serve him, is the center. All else we can if need be do without.

(3). Now we come to the type of packaging that is

specifically referred to in our text. For Christ is speaking here, above all, about *deceptive* wrappings.

I don't need to talk to houswives about the "giant size" packets that seem to shrink when the box is opened or to men about the gadgets that never live up to the promise on the cover or to children about the beautiful box of chocolate that *seemed* to have two layers but only had one. We all know that bright colors, fancy ribbons, gleaming cellophane can cover shoddy contents; and our wisdom is to discount the deceptive wrappings. What Jesus was saying here was: "Beware ye of the wrappings of the hypocrites." Hypocrisy is the wrapping we wear in order to appear to be better than we are. Those who are attacking our society today focus on hypocrisy as the besetting sin of what they call "the establishment." They would see in the deceptive wrappings in which so many of our goods are sold a symbol of our age — the age of packaging rather than of content.

There is hypocrisy, they say, in the Church. Sure; we plead guilty. Time and again we profess things that we have not truly practiced. We try to tell God this together every Sunday morning, but if we don't really mean it we fall into hypocrisy again. There is hypocrisy in government, in business, in family life. And there is hypocrisy among those who hurl the charge at others. For to accuse any man of hypocrisy is to set oneself on a pedestal where we know very well we do not belong.

Therefore, there is no word we should be less willing to use than this — unless we are looking into our hearts. Unless I have the purity, the insight, the perfection of Jesus Christ how can I look at my brother and call him a hypocrite? How do I know what his inmost desires are, what struggles are going on inside?

This is a word that each one of us must take for ourselves alone. And how soon we shall discover that we are all adept in deceptive packaging. What about the masks we wear? What one of us would contend that we always appear consistently as we really are? that we are exactly the same person in a room by ourselves, in our family, in our work, in church, in a crowded subway or driving a car? Some of the masks are harmless; some are quite unconscious; but some we assume simply because we want to be thought a certain kind of person. How difficult it is to be real, to be honest, to be consistent. We tend to package ourselves one way for our cronies, another way for strangers, yet another for someone we want to impress. It is even possible for us to keep a mask on when we are alone — if we ever really allow that to happen. In the parable of the Prodigal Son, Jesus shows what it is like for a man at long last to take the wrappings off, to drop the mask, for when this boy's supplies ran out and his cronies disappeared, "he came to himself." Real religion cannot begin for any of us until this happens. We must let the wrappings go and come to ourselves.

215

The Fall story in Genesis is the classic picture of the wrappings in which we try to hide from God. The communion with the Creator has been broken. "And Adam and his wife hid themselves from the presence of the Lord God amongst the trees of the garden." We've been there ever since. The trees are the symbol of the wrapping in which man hides from God. The famous fig leaf is the symbol of the wrapping in which we hide from one another. "Adam, where art thou?" This is the call we hear when we come to ourselves. The Prodigal heard it, you remember, and said: "I will arise and go to my Father." This is what living religion means. This is what the Gospel is about — the real presence of the Father and the awakening of the real you and the real me to respond. It only comes alive when the wrappings are off.

What Christ is saying to us in plain language is just this: Ultimately the wrappings will disappear. "For there is nothing covered, that shall not be revealed; neither hid, that shall not be known." Absolutely nothing can be hidden from God, and it is the real self that will out. In his solemn words to live with pretense will be hell, for hell is unreality. But to be always seeking to discard the wrappings — the impenetrable, the unnecessary and the deceptive — is to open our lives to the grace of heaven. For God is not looking for those who claim to be saints, but for sinners who ask nothing but his mercy. And they need have no fear.

216